Messages
from the
Heart
of
Love

Spirituality Basics in 144 Empowering Quotes

By Keith Higgs

Contents

Introduction   iv-vii

The Quotes   1-144

In Conclusion   145

Index   146-167

About the Author   168-169

Connections   170

Other Books by Keith Higgs   171-175

Introduction

Welcome to "Messages from the Heart of Love – Spirituality Basics in 144 Empowering Quotes" It's All About Love!

Since my earliest days of personal growth, I have found great power in quotes. A mentor suggested when reading a quote that speaks to me, I write it down and review it several times daily. This suggestion led to a collection of about 200 empowering quotes on little cards. I then read these quotes 2 or 3 times each day.

I eventually even recorded an audio copy of my quotes. I listened to them frequently whilst driving or before going to sleep.

We become what we think about! These powerful words became constant companions and a part of my belief systems, a part of me. They replaced many random thoughts that used to fly through my head. They were overwriting old beliefs with new thoughts. They were the foundation for further growth.

Collecting the most powerful quotes from my first book, much of which was channelled or gifted to me in the early hours of the morning, led to my second book, "The Little Book of Love - Quotes to Empower Your Journey Back to Love." This book is now successful. Over 6000 people follow and have liked its Facebook page. Some people enjoy using it as a part of their daily practice.

When I started sharing daily quotes from the book, to help publicise it, I also was collecting quote pictures that resonated with me.

After the Little Book of Love's quotes were all shared, I started looking for a new quote picture to share each day. I listened for a few words of wisdom to add to each picture to give meaning and clarification.

Even though this didn't lead to many book sales, Spirit encouraged me that I was giving back. People from over 100 countries were seeing the quotes daily.

I have received many positive responses. These daily messages are now seen by thousands. Some quotes have gone viral, and have been seen by over 20,000 people and shared over 100's of times.

I realised the book was already written. It just needed to be collected, compiled, and edited so that the power of some of these Loving messages could reach, inspire, and touch more people.

When you see a quote that speaks to you, I would highly recommend writing it down, collecting its wisdom, and letting it become a part of you.

Words of Power can cut through fears and bring healing and growth, especially when repeated as positive affirmations.

Use this book how it leads you. It's not designed just to be read straight through, there is also an index designed so you can research any particular topics that are speaking to you.

It can make a great gift, be a part of a daily practice, or even be left in a bathroom for moments of inspiration.

I pray that these words will speak to your heart, bring comfort and inspiration, and also it will help continue to further Our Oneness and Progress on this Magical Journey Back to Love.

I would Love to hear how these words speak to you. Send me a message. You can follow me and my books pages on Facebook to see more Inspiring Quotes. Contact details are later in the book.

Much Love Keith Higgs

As Within so Without.

Our Outer World is Created by and is a Picture or Representation of things that are Moving Within.

Change Comes from Within.

To Change our Circumstances and Outer Experiences, it is Necessary to Change Our Inner Thoughts and Beliefs.

This often takes Releasing and Letting go of any Past Traumas, False Beliefs, and Baggage from the Past.

It can be as Simple as Releasing something that no longer Serves, just Letting Go, or it may take some deeper work.

Either Way, Change is Possible.

Returning to the Love we are, is Our Destiny.

#Within #Without #Outer #World #Create #Picture
#Change #Circumstances #Experience #Possible
#Thoughts #Release #Return #Inner #Belief
#Past #Way #LetGo #Serve #Destiny
#Trauma #Baggage #Work

We Live for a Time in an Illusionary Temporary World.

All Things will Pass, Except Love which is Forever.

Love Yourself and Share Acts of Love.

Let Go All Heaviness of Heart and Hold Tight to Love.

Love will Grow, Its Magic Realm is being Created.

We will Ride with that Flow of Love into the Realm of Oneness, where All Love can be Found Again.

Yes, Real Love is Forever!

#Time #Illusion #Temporary #World #AllThings
#Forever #SelfLove #Share #LetGo #Hold #Heart
#Flow #Live #Growth #Act #Magic #Realm
#Yourself #Create #Ride #Oneness #Found

Our Heart also has a Mind!

Leave Behind the Old Automatic Mind Programs that No Longer Serve you, or Rewrite them.

They were Installed to Protect us as Children by a System and Parents that often Knew nothing better.

Drop into Our Heart, Listen to its Mind, Make the Choices, and Find Beliefs that Empower the You of Today.

Love is Leading the Way, and Will Create a New World with Us.

#Heart #Mind #Automatic #Programs #Serve
#Rewrite #Protect #Children #Parents #Listen
#Choice #Find #Belief #Empower #Today
#Leading # #Way #Create #World

What Am I Thinking About?

Are my Thoughts Creating the World I Desire?

Our Experience is Created by Our Thoughts.

Focusing Thought, especially from the Heart, is a Powerful Tool of Creation.

I am at Choice and the Creator of My Reality.

I Design my Thoughts.

Let's Paint Our World with Bright Colours and Connecting Experiences with the Brush of Love.

#Thoughts #Thinking #World #Desire #Tool
#Experience #Focus #Thought #Reality #Heart
#Choice #Create #Creator #Reality #Design
#Powerful #Connection

Let Out Your Inner Animal.

We have Created an often Pristine World, Suppressing much that is considered too Wild or Too Messy.

Let's Love, Accept and Play with All Parts of Us.

Suppressing Our Nature and Wild Desires can lead to missing many of the Joys and Freedoms of our Human Experience.

Shadows can cause many problems if not Accepted, Recognised, and Loved back into Our Oneness.

Yes, Do All Things in Love, but don't Cage any of the Aspects of our Divine Nature.

\# Inner #Animal #Create #World #Acceptance #Play #Parts #Nature #Desire #Lead #Joy #Freedom #Human #Experience #Aspect #AllThings #Shadows #Cause #Recognise #Problems #Oneness #Divine

Become the Observer.

Am I the Thoughts that Fly through my Head?

Am I the Emotions that sweep through my Body?

These are a Shared Part of Being Human, but I don't have to Keep or Hold Onto these often Crazy Experiences.

Let Emotions Flow-through otherwise they can get Stuck and cause problems.

Choose Empowering Thoughts, Keep them as Beliefs and Affirmations, Let all others Fly on By.

As the Pilot for this Earthly Journey, I can make Choices.

#Become #Observer #Thoughts #Head #Body
#Emotions #Being #Part #Human #Crazy #Flow
#Others #Experience #Stuck #Problems #HoldOn
#Hold #Empower #Thoughts #Cause #Journey
#Affirmations #Belief #Pilot #Earthly #Choice

What am I Doing to Help Change My World?

Yes, Inner Work and Self Love are Vitally Important. There also Comes a Time when Giving Back and Sharing that Love is also very Important.

Love isn't designed to be just for Self, it's about Giving, Loving, Service, Relationships for Healing, and Discovering Our Oneness.

These things are also absolutely Needed for Continued Growth.

We are Called to be Creators of the New in so many ways.

Find that Calling, and Share it with Love.

#Doing #Help #Change #World #Inner #Work #SelfLove #Important #Giving #Service #Relationship #Healing #Time #Discovering #Oneness #Design #Growth #Create #Find #Ways #Calling #Share

Thoughts Create Things.

Everything in Our World was First Created by Thought.

Energy Follows Intention.

What Will Your Thoughts Create Today?

Change Old Thought Patterns, Disempowering Beliefs, and Release Stuck Energy to Change Our World.

Image In, All Desired Changes.

Transformation is an Inside Job.

#Thoughts #Create #World #Energy #Intention #Patterns #Disempowering #Change #Belief #Today #Release #Stuck #Energy #Desire #Transformation #Inside

Remember, Life works through Cycles.

If you are Feeling Stuck, Down, or Troubled by Present Circumstances, take Heart, they will Change, Hold On.

A New Dawn is Coming. Love's Sun will Return.

Let Go of all Past Hurts, Resentments, and any Lingering Cold from Winters Storms.

Every Day is a New Opportunity.

Live, Love and Dance in the Coming Sunshine.

#Remember #Cycles #Life #Stuck #Troubled #Work #Circumstances #Heart #Change #HoldOn #Dawn #Return #LetGo #Past #Hurts #Change #Resentments #Winters #Storms #Feelings #Live #Sun #Opportunity #Dance #Coming #Sunshine

Love has a Plan and a Promise.
Everything will be Okay.
Fear Not!

Even when in the Midst of the Darkest Night, Know that the Triumphant End of Our Story is Already Written.

Our Birthright and Destiny is the Return to Our Natural State of Love and the Creation of a New Paradise.

Hold On, Accept, Love and Forgive, Yourself and All others, It is Soon Coming.

Get Ready!

#Plan #Promise #Fear #Night #Know #Triumph
#Story #Birthright #Destiny #Return #Creation
#State #Paradise #Dark #HoldOn #Acceptance
#Yourself #Others #Forgive #Coming

Hold on and Believe.

The Fire is Burning to Purify, not to Destroy.

The Alchemist Melts Gold over the Fire to bring out anything that is not Fine Gold.

Fear Not!

Our Divine Nature, Like the Phoenix, will Rise from All Seeming Ashes of Defeat.

Our Heart is Forever Pure, we are just Leaving Behind things no longer needed for our Journey.

Love is Calling Us Home.

#HoldOn #Believe #Fire #Burn #Purify
#Alchemist #Melt #Fear #Divine #Rise
#Defeat #Heart #Forever #Pure
#Nature #Journey #Calling #Home

Take an Inventory.

What are the Fears, Thoughts, and Beliefs that no longer Serve me?

These are not mine, they are Baggage collected from others, often during difficult experiences in childhood.

Overwrite them with New Empowering Thoughts and Beliefs.

Make Choices that are in alignment with Love, which is Our Core Being.

I am in Control of my Life and Choose Love as my Path and Destination.

#Inventory #Fear #Thoughts #Belief #Serve
#Baggage #Difficult #Experience #Childhood
#Control #Choice #Core #Being #Life #Empower
#Destination #Being #Others #Overwrite #Path

In Times of Seeming
Darkness, it's so Important
to Let Our Love Shine.

One Look of Love, a Smile,

a Hug, an Act of Love can
Change an entire World.

Let Love Flow without
measure and Know it Always,
eventually flows back.

The Magic of Love is,
It's Impossible to truly
give it away!

How will You Share
Love today?

♥ ♥ ♥ ♥ ♥ ♥ ♥ ♥

#Times #Darkness Important #Act #Shine #Smile
#Hug #Look #Change #World #Flow #Without
#Know #Today #Magic #Impossible #Give #Share

Let Go of the Fear of Death and Live.

Our Core Being is Pure Energy, which is Indestructible.

Fear Not, for Death is just Passing into another Realm.

Life, which is Forever, and the Higher Being, which we are, have a Perfect Plan.

Trust and Live to the Full.

Our Only Judge is Ourself, so be Sure to Love, Get to Know, and Forgive Yourself.

Remember the Divine Being You are.

#Energy #Death #LetGo #Fear #Perfect #Core
#Being #Pure #Indestructible #Know #Passing
#Forever #Plan #Trust #Judge #Divine #Yourself
#Live #Life #Realm #Forgiveness #Remember

Leave the Past Behind.

The Memories that are Left have almost certainly become so Distorted by Time that they are quite a different picture than what actually happened.

Old Patterns of Thought Magnifying either the Failures or the Perfection, neither are completely true.

Wash all, with Forgiveness of Self and any others involved.

Then Invest your Energy in Creating the New and Enjoying the Now.

#Past #Memories #Become #Time #Patterns
#Thought #Picture #Failure #Perfection #Truth
#Wash #Forgiveness #Others #Self #Energy
#True #Enjoy #Create #Now

Life can Appear to be Tough

However, Most Obstacles and seemingly Bad events are the seeds of Growth.

We have Inner Resources and Strength that will help us through Everything.

All things work together for Good for All who Love and we are Love.

Trust Yourself and your Inner Strength, All is Forever Well.

Life's Troubles are Just a Passing Storm in a Temporary Dream.

They will make us Stronger.

Look for the Silver Lining.

#Trust #Life #Appear #Tough #Obstacles
#Dream #AllThings #Events #Seeds #Growth
#Resources #Work #Help #Good #Strength
#Forever #Look #Troubles #Inner #Passing
#Storm #Temporary #Yourself

Watch for the Mystery.

Listen for the Breath of Spirit.

Explore New Ways and Dimensions.

Look Within through the Heart Portal.

There are Realms of Spirit beyond our Normal Senses.

Ask, Stop, Look, and Listen.

Discover the Love, which is the Foundation of All.

#Watch #Mystery #Breath #Spirit #Explore
#Ways #Look #Within #Heart #Portal #Realm
#Normal #Senses #Ask #Stop #Listen
#Beyond #Discover

Fall in Love with Love.

Have You Discovered the Beloved Within?

Much of the Nature we See in Our Outer World is composed of Pictures and Expressions of Love.

These are Signs and Pointers to the Greatest Truths. Our World is Composed of Love.

Let Yourself become Drunk with Love and Discover her Mysteries and Ever Present Presence.

#Discover #Beloved #Within #Signs #Truth
#Outer #World #Pictures #Become #Yourself
#Drunk #See #Nature #Mysteries

Love is the Portal

**It's Our Gateway back to Our
True Self and Our Home.**

Here is a Simple Exercise.

Think of a Time You were Loved.

**Stand, Meditate and Rest in that
Feeling for awhile.**

**Let Go of all else and Let its
Energy Flow.**

**Then from that Place of Heart,
Ask your Question, Let the
Healing Flow, or Send
your Prayer.**

**That Love is All-Powerful when
we Believe and Enter its Portal.**

#Portal #Gateway #TrueSelf #Home #Time
#Meditate #Rest #Feelings #LetGo #Energy
#Flow #Place #Heart #Ask #Question #Powerful
#Healing #Prayer #Believe #Enter

Whatever Life throws,

Take a few Moments before Reacting or Responding.

Our Peace is Precious, Don't let it be Stolen too easily.

Look at all sides.

Most Actions and Attitudes are Nothing about us but are caused by Fears and Deep Wounds from Previous Experiences.

Staying Calm in the Heat of the Moment is Love.

Take those moments to ask, What would Love do?

#Calm #Life #Moments #React #Response
#Peace #Look #Action #Attitude #Cause #Fear
#Wounds #Experience #Ask

Hold on to that Dream,
Keep Believing, even in the Darkest Moments.

The Darkest moment can be just before Dawn when it seems like that Light is Never coming, yet it always does!

That Moment, when we Don't Give up, can be the turning point. Persistence Pays.

Those Magic Moments when Life checks if we Believe can change Everything.

Be Sure of Your Truth and Hold On!

#HoldOn #Dream #Believe #Dark #Moments
#Dawn #Light #Coming #Persistence #Magic
#Life #Change #Truth

When You Have Questions, Look Inside.

There are Many Sources of Wisdom, Ponder in Your Divine Heart.

Ask Spirit and Your Guides Within.

Look from Different Perspectives.

In the Oneness, Great Wisdom is waiting to be Found.

Seek, and You will Find.

Ask, and You will Receive.

Love has the Answers and will Guide.

#Question #Look #Inside #Sources #Wisdom
#Found #Divine #Heart #Spirit #Oneness
#Seek #Find #Within #Ask #Receive
#Answers #Guide

Let Your Love Expand.

Love is Far Greater than Individual Relationships, which can, of course, be a Powerful Place for Healing when kept Sacred.

However, Love is far Greater than Relationship with just One other.

Real Love Expands Past All Boundaries and Takes Us into the Oneness.

Love is in Relationship with All.

Let Your Love Grow, Share and Live Love to Discover its Wonders.

#Expand #Relationship #Place #Powerful
#Healing #Boundaries #Oneness #Past #Growth
#Share #Live #Discover #Wonders

Look Inside!

Why Look into the Mirror of a Darkening World when the Source of all Light is Hidden Deep Within?

Yes, there are Signs, Pictures, and Truths there to be found, but the Source of our Love is Within.

Commune in the Temple of Our Heart.

Loves Answers will Shine through.

Clarity and Purpose can be found Deep Within.

#Look #Inside #Mirror #Dark #World #Source #Light #Hidden #Within #Signs #Pictures #Truth #Commune #Heart #Shine #Found #Answers #Purpose

Step Out of Routine
and the Normal.

Take Time to Breathe,
Explore New Places, New
People, New Experiences.

Stretch the Comfort Zone,
otherwise, you could find it
Shrinking.

Life is a Gift to Live.

It's a Realm to Discover Our
Purpose, Passions and Loves.

We are Voyagers on an
Exciting Journey Back
to Love.

#Experience #Routine #Normal #Time #Breath
#Explore #Places #ComfortZone #Shrinking #Life
#Gift #Live #Realm #Discover #Purpose #Find
#Passions #Journey

We Operate on Autopilot much of the Time.

Old Beliefs have created Automatic Responses to many Repeating Situations that Neural Pathways in our Brains Guide us down.

The Question, Do these Serve the now, Adult you, of Today?

Observe the Patterns and Pause, Interrupt those that no longer Serve.

You can make New Choices. Becoming Aware is a Great Start.

Rewrite the Old with Empowering New Beliefs, Affirmations, and Practices.

#Patterns #Pause #Autopilot #Automatic #Time
#Repeat #Responses #Situations #Choice
#NeuralPathways #Now #Question #Practices
#Serve #Observe #Aware #Rewrite #Empower
#Today #Guide #Create #Belief #Affirmations

There is Magic in Acceptance.

Acceptance of All Feelings, even those that have been pushed away.

Acceptance of All Sickness, if it is in My World somehow it is also in me.

Acceptance of All Sadness, if it is in the World then it is also in me.

Acceptance of Our Many States, this can Cleanse All.

The Magic is that Acceptance brings Healing, Wholeness, and Oneness Again.

Let Go and Let Love Bring Her Powerful Magic and Reign.

#Acceptance #Feelings #Sickness #World
#Sadness #States #Cleansing #Healing
#Wholeness #Oneness #LetGo #Powerful
#Magic #Reign

We Are Love,
which is the Seeding Essence of Miracles.

We are Alchemists, Our Art to Turn Everything into Love.

Miracles are Love's Manifestation on Earth.

From the Place of Love, let Desires Flow.

All Things are Possible when mixed in Loves Crucible, especially when the Power of Two is applied.

The Power of Love can Transform even our Earthly World.

Be that Love.

#Miracles #Seeds #Essence #Alchemist #Art
#AllThings #Manifestation #Power #Transform
#Possible #Place #Desire #Flow #Earthly #World

For Our Growth to Progress,
it's Important to Look at all Inner Thoughts, Attitudes, and Experiences.

Lurking in our Semi-Consciousness are often Shames, Blames, Regrets, and Rejected Parts of Ourselves.

To Reach Peace and Wholeness, it's Important to Reconcile and Reconnect with All these, Disowned Parts and Experiences.

Acceptance is the Key, Blended with Self Love and Forgiveness.

Let's bring all Parts and Memories back into the Oneness of Love.

#Growth #Progress #Important #Inner #Thought #Attitude #Experience #Consciousness #Shame #Blame #Regret #Parts #Peace #Key #SelfLove #Wholeness #Reconcile #Acceptance #Oneness #Ourselves #Forgiveness #Memories

Watch and Listen.

We have Guides and Inner Voices that are Helping us on Our Journey through Life.

Know, in Spite of Life's, Sometimes Seeming Opposing Circumstances, You are Deeply Loved.

There is Always Help, Support, and Guidance available.

Look Inside, Ask for Help, it can come in many forms.

Life and Spirit Love Us.

Our Eventual Destiny is Assured.

#Life #Watch #Listen #Guide #Inner #Voice #Journey #Know #Circumstances #Help #Support #Guidance #Look #Inside #Spirit #Ask #Destiny #Assured

Let's Ask to See Life with Eyes of Spirit.

Opening Our Third Eye can Reveal a World of Oneness, of Connection, the Relationship of All Things, and the Harmony of Energies Flowing.

Let's Look past the vision of the temporary world that our Mind has created in its desire for Separate Supremacy.

Living in Our Heart and Holding its Vision of the Love We Are, will speed our Return Home.

#Ask #See #Life #Spirit #Reveal #Oneness
#Connection #Relationship #AllThings #Harmony
#Look #Energy #Flow #Heart #Vision #Temporary
#Past #Create #Ask #Eyes #Desire #World #Mind
#Opening #Hold #Separate #Return #Home

Look at Life through the Eyes of the Heart, there all Truths and Beauty can be seen.

Our Physical Eyes and World can often Deceive with Pictures and Fears from a Decaying Illusionary World.

Remember, in this world, nothing is Permanent, but the Love in our Hearts.

Let that Love Create Connections and Relationships which surpass all Time and Space.

Love's Realm is being Created in the Here and Now.

#Look #Life #Eyes #Heart #Truth #Physical
#Pictures #World #Fear #Illusion #Create
#Connection #Relationship #Time
#Remember #Realm #Now

Dive from the Mind into the World of Feelings.

Observe all that would Flow through.

Listen to the Body, it has much to Share.

Watch, and Explore the Natural World.

Nature has many Pictures and Deep Truths, Hidden in Plain Sight.

There are Signposts, Answers, and Directions for every Question when we Pause to Listen.

Let Our Heart lead back into the Joy of Being the Love We Forever Are.

#Feelings #Mind #Observe #Flow #Listen #Body
#Nature #Pictures #Truth #Hidden #Lead #Pause
#Signposts #Answers #Direction #Being #Watch
#Question #Explore #Pause #Share
#World #Heart #Joy #Forever

The Days of Learning are ending.

The Minds Constant Quest for Knowledge can never be Fully Satisfied.

Yet, In the Oneness of Our Heart, in Love, there is a Place of Knowing and Understanding.

We are Entering a Realm where All will become Clear.

We will Know as we are Known.

Remembering the Love we are is One of the first steps on this Path.

#Learning #Ending #Know #Understanding #Mind
#Constant #Quest #Oneness #Heart #Place
#Clear #Enter #Realm #Become
#Remember #Steps #Path

Explore Your Hidden Power.

We have Powers that are Undiscovered, Forgotten, and Unused, especially the Power to Manifest.

Nothing is Missing, though it may not yet have appeared in our Physical World.

Ask in Love and Belief, for All it takes to Manifest the Perfection of your Being and all True Desires of our beautiful Heart.

Love is the Power of the Universe, and that Love is Forever on our Side.

#Explore #Hidden #Power #Forgotten #Ask
#Manifest #Physical #World #Appear #Belief
#Perfection #Forever #Being #True #Desire
#Heart #Universe

At the End of Each Day,
Review and Clean any Chords of Connection that may have been Left in Disarray.

Energetically send Love and Forgiveness to Self and all Others.

Let Go of Hurts and Misunderstandings and anything that disturbs the Peace of the Love you are.

The Poison from Grudges will eat up all the resources Spirit has.

Life is too Precious to spend time holding onto the weights of Discord.

Forgive and Let Go, lest it Dim the Light we need in this Seemingly Darkening World.

#Forgiveness #LetGo #Healing #Growth
#Review #Life #Connection #Poison #Grudges
#Resources #Hurts #Peace #Others #Spirit
#Weights #Time #Self #Light #Dark #World

Listen.

The Voice of Love is waiting patiently for us to Stop, Look, and Listen.

There are Many Messages, they surround us with their Truths, yet how often do we Pause to Listen?

Nature cries in its Silence.

Open your Senses and see the Circle of Life.

In the depth of our Heart, all Truth is waiting for Our Attention.

Let Love be Our Guide.

Her Realm is Calling us Home.

#Listen #Voice #Stop #Look #Messages
#Truth #Nature #Open #Senses #Pause
#Life #Heart #Attention #See #Guide
#Realm #Calling #Home

Share Your Love,
Your Touch, Your Hugs, they will Bring Healing.

Where two agree, Touching anything, it shall be done.

Babies thrive with Touch and Shrivel without it, adults too!

Healing comes through Giving and Receiving, in fact, it is impossible to give without receiving.

During these times, when it seems everything conspires to stop our touch and sharing Love, let's look for more ways to be that Love.

#Share #Touch #Hugs #Healing #Give
#Impossible #Receive #Connection #Agree
#Without #Times #Stop #Look #Ways

If You knew what you have always wanted to Be, Do, Have, or Experience, what would it be?

Have you ever Dared to take the time to consider that?

Capture that Dream, write it in Your Heart and on paper or a journal.

Now Look at and Imagine ways it could happen.

Dreaming and Imagination are the first steps to Creation.

Leave the fears behind and Live.

Know, All things are Possible for those who Love.

Just Believe.

#Dream #Want #Desire #Do #Know #Imagination #Possible #Experience #Dare #Write #Heart #Creation #Time #Fear #Look #Live #AllThings #Ways #Believe #Steps

After the Fire, After the Purging, there is Only Love.

In the Refining Pot, Gold is heated until the Dross, and everything that is not Pure Gold rises to the top and is pushed out.

Our Trials are sent to help us realise and release All that is not Love.

Look not, at Trials as Chastisement, they are the Kiss of Purifying Love.

The Moth loves the Light more than even its Life.

As Warriors, we agreed to this Journey.

It is Our Return to Love.

#Fire #Return #Purging #Refining #Gold #Rise
#Pure #Look #Trials #Help #Realise #Release
#Life #Kiss #Purifying #Light #Agree #Journey

Loves Sees through the Illusions and past the Hurts, Scars, and Wounds.

Love Sees through Walls, built to protect Our Hearts.

Love Knows, Within all Beings, sometimes well hidden, there Lives a part of Ourself.

Our Parts are Seemingly Scattered for awhile, Playing Games of Separation.

Yet in Truth, Oneness is the Only Reality, as Love is Forever Whole.

Time will End, and we will once again Discover the Divine Being and Beings we have Always Known.

#Past #Illusion #Hurts #Wounds #Walls #Protect
#Discover #Heart #Within #Being #Hidden
#Play #Games #Divine #Separation #Truth
#Reality #Oneness #Forever #Whole #Part
#Live #Know #Time

Life's Plan is Unfolding Perfectly.

There are No Accidents.

As tough as it may sometimes seem, I hold the Belief that Love and I am in Control and Create everything in my Life.

This Belief gives the Power to affect Change, at Cause, rather than being controlled and dominated by the winds of change.

We are in control of a Path and Plan, created by Our Love in a time before time.

That Love is Gently Guiding us all Back Home, and also sometimes pulling us out of the mire created by our thoughts.

#Life #Plan #Unfolding #Perfect #Belief #Give #Control #Create #Cause #Change #Path #Time #Time #Power #Guide #Home #Thoughts

Healing, like everything, is a Choice.

Our Greatest Power, and I feel Life's Purpose, is to make Choices.

What do I really want?

Some find more Comfort in their sickness. Others find Lessons in the Challenge.

Life's Plan is Growth and Being All we can Be, bringing many kinds of Fruit.

Choosing to hold tight to the Love we are will bring back Knowing and Understanding on this Journey into the Mystery.

#Healing #Choice #Power #Feelings #Purpose
#Sickness #Lessons #Life #Plan #Growth #Fruit
#Others #Understanding #Find #Know #Being
#Want #Journey #Mystery

Be Kind! Who Too?

Everyone and Especially Ourself.

Let's Stop Stop Beating Ourselves Up!

What we would never tolerate if applied to Others, we frequently do to Ourselves.

Self Castigation, Self Belittling, Self Hate. STOP IT!

Let's have Self Love, Understanding, Mercy, and if needed, Forgiveness.

Our True Self is Pure, though often Scarred from many Sad Experiences.

Resurrect it with Love, Kindness and Understanding.

Bring it Back into the Oneness of Love with the Acceptance and Compassion You'd give to Another.

#Kindness #SelfLove #Belittling #Ourselves
#Stop #Others #Mercy #Hate #Understanding
#Forgiveness #Pure #Experience #Oneness
#TrueSelf #Acceptance #Compassion #Give

Happiness is a Choice.

Why then do I frequently choose Paths leading through Fears to Sadness and Separation?

We are in Spirit All One, yet sometimes I make Loneliness my home rather than Exploring, Oneness, Relationship, and Connection.

What strangely perverse part of me is holding me back from the Joy's of Heavens Realms.

I Vow to Heal those wounds and wash away the fears with the Balm of Love.

The time for Love's return is Now.

#Happiness #Choice #Path #Oneness #Hold
#Sadness #Separation #Relationship #Healing
#Part #Connection #Joy #Heaven #Realm
#Wash #Fear #Time #Loneliness #Spirit
#Leading #Wounds #Return

Life is a Miracle.

From a Tiny Seed, almost nothing, Bursts forth an Amazing Power, a Drive to Create, to Become.

We are that Power of Life, Driven to Fulfil Our Destiny.

We are here to Create the New and Change Our World with Love.

That Seed is Unstoppable it will Become All that is Intended.

Relax, Trust and Watch Your Miracle Unfold, it's Your Destiny.

#Life #Miracle #Seed #Amazing #Power
#Drive #Create #Become #Destiny
#Change #World #Intention #Relax
#Trust #Watch #Unfolding

Let's Explore the Depth of Love
from Every Part of Our Being.

Experience Love from
each Chakra.

Cycle through them,
breathing slowly.

Meditate on the Feeling of
Love Flowing Out.

Know that it is Flowing Back
in Equal Measure.

It's Impossible, in Spirit, to
Give Love Away.

We are Love and as We
Awaken, will Dance in that
Love Forever.

#Explore #Part #Being #Experience #Chakras
#Breath #Slow #Meditate #Flow #Impossible
#Spirit #Give #Awakening #Dance
#Feelings #Forever

Our Mind is Constantly Struggling for the Feelings of Certainty and Control.

These things are Impossible within the boundaries of this Earthly Plane.

Here All is Illusion that eventually crumbles back into dust.

Yet in Spirit, through the Heart Portal, there is a State of Knowing, of Destiny, and a Realm where Love is Forever.

Set Your Heart Seeking that Place, where once again All will Rest, Love, and Play in Peace.

#Certainty #Control #Illusion #Mind #Constant #Struggling #Feelings #Spirit #Heart #Portal #State #Realm #Know #Play #Forever #Seeking #Impossible #Within #Rest #Earthly #Destiny #Place #Peace #Boundaries

Whenever Sorrow Comes,
Accept Her, Embrace Her, and then Let Her Go.

When the Tears Come, don't fight with them, Let them Wash You.

In Due Time, Be sure to Release her.

She has others to touch with her melting Powers.

Don't get stuck in that State forever. Emotions must be Released to work their Magic.

The Walls around Our Hearts must be washed away so we can be Reunited in Love.

#Sorrow #Acceptance #Embrace #LetGo
#Tears #Wash #Release #Others #Power
#State #Forever #Emotions #Work #Magic
#Walls #Touch #Time #Stuck #Heart #Reunite

In Spirit, Everything is in Relationship.

We are a Part, and Also the Whole of a Wonderful Cosmic Pattern of Evolving Love.

Each Part is Magically Connected to Every Other.

Our Heart Yearns for True Relationship, which is for Healing and Reconnecting in Oneness.

Cultivate the Cords of Love, for they are the Guides Calling us Home.

#Relationship #Spirit #Part #Whole #Wonder
#Pattern #Evolving #Magic #Connection #Heart
#True #Healing #Reconnect #Oneness
#Guide #Calling #Home

Our Human Mind and Desire is for Certainty, yet Spirit often works Miracles in the Place of Uncertainty and Flow.

The Lesson can be to Trust the Process and Let Go of all Expectations.

Then Life has the Opportunity to Create its Magic in the Wonder of Now.

Rejoice in the Unknown and Open to all Possibilities.

Rest in the Knowing of Life's Perfect Plan and Love.

#Human #Unknown #Certainty #Works #Miracles
#Place #Flow #Lesson #Mind #Trust #Process
#Magic #Now #Desire #Life #Opportunity #Create
#Wonder #Now #Rejoice #Possibilities #LetGo
#Spirit #Rest #Open #Know #Perfect #Plan

Do You Recognise and Appreciate Yourself?

Do You See the Magnificent Divine Being Within?

Have you Found and Embraced Your True Self and Shed all Lies, Old Patterns, and Thoughts that attempt to convince you otherwise?

Can You Love Yourself and Dance in the Joy of Knowing the Divine, You Are?

It's Possible!

Open, Melt, and Let Go. Love is Carrying us Home.

#Recognise #Appreciate #Yourself #Divine #Being #Within #Found #Embrace #TrueSelf #Patterns #Thoughts #Dance #Joy #Open #See #Knowing #Possible #Melt #LetGo #Home

The Mind Screams and Holds Tightly to it's Imposed Identity of Separate Being.

Our Heart Lives Forever, in Our Original State of Oneness.

Let's Claim and Live in Moments of Respite, from the Constant Whirring of the Ever Busy Mind.

Love Calls us to Peace and Reunification of all Parts of us that the Earthly Mind Excludes.

Just a short while Longer, the Battle Rages.

Love's Victory and Reign is Soon.

#Mind #Hold #Separate #Being #Heart #Live #State #Forever #Oneness #Moments #Earthly #Battle #Parts #Constant #Peace #Victory #Reign #Busy

It's Possible to Change Our Experience!

What are You Looking For?

What are You Thinking About?

What are You Vibrating?

Which Patterns are Constantly Recurring?

Recognise and Make Changes to Anything that no longer Serves.

Imprint New Thoughts, Affirmations, and Beliefs.

If Needed Ask for the Help to Change Your World.

Life's Plan is to Recreate Paradise for us All.

#Possible #Change #Experience #Looking
#Help #Thinking #Vibrating #Patterns
#Constant #Serve #Recurring #Recognise
#Imprint #Affirmations #Thoughts #Belief
#Life #World #Plan #Ask #Paradise

Step into the Magic of Now.

**There Supposed Little
Things can become a Place
to Dance in Wonder.**

**Jump into a Smile,
or Share one.**

**There the Gap between Our
Universes can Narrow, and True
Connection can be Found.**

**Discover Our Oneness, far
from Regrets from the Past,
or Fears of the Future.**

**Enter the Heart of Love. it is
the Bridge to a Forever Now.**

#Now #Magic #Become #Place #Dance #Wonder
#Smile #Share #Universe #True #Connection
#Found #Oneness #Regret #Discover #Past
#Fear #Future #Heart #Forever

What can I Turn into Love Today?

At Times I Encounter, Excluded, Unaccepted Parts of Me.

Maybe those Parts, from Within, come to Dance in my Outer World, so that I can Recognise them and bring them back into the Oneness of Love.

Acceptance is the Key.

I am Responsible for Everything in My World.

It's All my Creation.

Anything other than this can lead to Feelings of being a Victim.

I'm Sorry, Please Forgive me, Thank you, I Love You.

Let's Turn this World back into Love.

#Today #Encounter #Excluded #Unaccepted
#Parts #Dance #Within #Recognise #Oneness
#Feelings #Outer #World #Acceptance #Key
#Responsible #Lead #Feelings #Being #Creation
#Times #Sorry #Forgiveness

Seek Love.

Not Just Human Love, though that is Great when it is True.

Seek to Know Divine Love, which is Everything.

Seek to Know Unconditional Love, which can produce many Tears.

Those Tears Wash & bring Deep Cleansing and Healing.

Seek to Find Our True Self, which is that Love.

That Love will bring us Home.

#Seek #Human #Picture #Divine
#Unconditional #Tears #Wash #Cleansing
#Healing #Find #TrueSelf #Home

Change Your Inner State
to Change the Outer Experience.

Wrap the Inner World in the Desired States.

Choose to Be Happy, To Feel Peace even in a Storm.

To Know Love, even in times of Loneliness.

There is Always Love Inside, and We are Forever Safe.

Think of times of Love and Let them Permeate your Beautiful Heart.

We Can Create our World and Experience with Imagination, Visualisation, and Calling in from our Vast Resources the Essence of the Love We Are.

#Change #Inner #State #Experience #Happiness
#Peace #Storm #Times #Loneliness #Inside
#Forever #Outer #Safe #Feelings #Heart #Create
#World #Imagination #Desire #Visualisation
#Calling #Know #Resources #Essence

The Time of Teaching and Teachers is Ending.

The Time of Discovery Within and Knowing is Now.

Let's Become Signposts to the Joy, Peace, and Love Within, Sharing by Sample and Osmosis.

Just Being Love is Enough.

Love will Permeate All when Lived in Truth.

Love's Realm will Fill Our Earth.

#Time #Teach #Teachers #Ending #Discover
#Within #Knowing #Now #Become #Now #Joy
#Signposts #Sharing #Peace #Being
#Enough #Live #Truth #Realm #Earth

Trust the Process!

We are Life's Unfolding Plan.

Life Creates in Perfection.

Look at Our Amazing Universe, Everything has its Purpose.

All are part of the Circling Dance of Life.

Love is Manifesting and Experiencing itself.

We are that Love and will soon Forget our Imaginary Differences and Reunite in Oneness, which in Truth we never left.

#Trust #Process #Unfolding #Plan #Life
#Create #Perfection #Universe #Purpose #Part
#Dance #Amazing #Manifestation #Experience
#Reunite #Look #Forget #Oneness #Truth

It's Time to take a Different Look and Experience.

Old Beliefs Wired our Neural Pathways and Created Our Supposed Reality.

Rewire them with New Perceptions, Beliefs, and Practices.

All Things are Possible.

What kind of World would you Like to Create?

What do you Desire?

Love will Lead the Way.

#Time #Look #Perception #Rewire #Belief
#Lead #NeuralPathways #Practices #Reality
#Create #AllThings #Experience #World
#Desire #Possible #Way

Watch for the Signs.

Experience and Study Nature.

Within her Beauty are so many Pictures and Demonstrations of Our Journey through Life.

If you'd like to Understand more, leave the hubbub and confusion of the city behind and commune in the Garden of Life.

Watch even the tiniest plant pushing out from its Seed, facing the Sun, and drawing energy from both Light and Earth in its Quest to bring forth Fruit.

Let's drop back to our Roots and Discover Our Love in the Sky and the Earth.

#Watch #Signs #Within #Experience #Nature
#Picture #Understand #Confusion #Sun
#Commune #Journey #Life #Seed #Light #Quest
#Energy #Earth #Fruit #Discover #Roots

My Inner Changes, Change My World.

Struggling in the Perceived Outer World Only Creates More Struggle.

Changes come from Inner Work.

To Change my World, I Change my Life.

Let Go, and Let the Love from your Heart Manifest ever Outward.

Be the Change you Desire.

#Change #Inner #World #Create #Work
#Outer #Struggle #Perception #LetGo #Life
#Heart #Manifest #Desire

It's Time to Move from Mind Dominated Thoughts
to the Place of Love Inspired Feelings.

Let Our Heart Rule.

Its Love Inspired Wisdom will Lead us Back Home.

This is Awakening.

Change is Coming and is Necessary.

Let Go of Old Ways and Let Spirit Flow.

The Love in Our Hearts Lives Forever.

#Time #Move #Awakening #Mind #Thoughts
#Heart #Feelings #Place #Inspired #Wisdom
#Lead #Home #Change #LetGo #Coming #Spirit
#Ways #Flow #Live #Forever

Switch on Your Light.

Live Love!

Love wants to Use us to Create the New World of Love.

Within, we have Individual Gifts to Discover that will Touch Others.

Listen to Our Heart it Will Lead.

Seek and Share Your Gifts.

Maybe Someone or Maybe Many Await Your Light.

Let Love Shine through You.

#Light #Live #Want #Heart #Lead #Create
#World #Gifts #Discover #Touch #Others
#Listen #Seek #Within #Share #Shine

We are in the Process of Awakening.

It is moving from Earthly Minds through Our Heart Portal into Oneness.

It's Remembering Our Divinity and Discovering again Our True Self.

There is Healing, on the Journey, from the many Traumas of Life.

The Ending is Inevitable the Time it takes can depend on our Choices and Flow.

Letting go of the Struggle and Dropping into Flow can make for a much easier ride.

Love is Carrying us All Home.

#Awakening #Earthly #Mind #Heart #Remember
#Oneness #Portal #Divinity #Discover #TrueSelf
#Time #Ride #Healing #Journey #Trauma #LetGo
#Ending #Life #Struggle #Choice #Flow #Home

Trust Life!

Sometimes it can seem all Hope is Lost, there are Disappointments, Grief, and Shattered Dreams on every side.

It seems like the End.

Yet, Know that Life Loves you and has a Plan, even if you can't see it yet.

Hold on, let the Emotions pass through, in due time Love will Surprise you, and Joy will return.

The Sun always Rises even after the Darkest nights.

#Trust #Life #Hope #Lost #Disappointment
#Grief #Dream #HoldOn #Emotions #Sunrise
#Time #See #Rise #Know #Joy #Return
#Sun #Dark #Plan #Night

Here is the Mystery.

There is in Each of Us a Place which is All of Us.

It could be called the Heart of Being.

It is the Essence of Love, The Oneness, The Divine.

It Sings through every Mountain Stream, every Flower, and every Sunrise.

Nature Shares Its Delights.

It is where the Unknown Enters Our World and Becomes Known.

Stop Look and Listen Today.

How do You Experience Love?

#Mystery #Place #Heart #Being #Essence
#Oneness #Divine #Flower #Sun #Nature
#Unknown #Enter #World #Become #Know
#Stop #Look #Listen #Today #Experience

What Would You Like to Experience More of?

If you Desire more Love, Be and Vibrate Love.

Love Yourself, Love Life, Live in Gratitude, that Frequency will attract More of the Same.

We are in Essence, Energy Vibrating.

What Frequency are Your Frequent Thoughts Creating?

Are You Desiring Change?

Change Your Thoughts and thus your Actions.

That Will Change Your Life!

#Experience #Desire #Vibrate #Frequency #Live
#Attract #Essence #Energy #Thoughts #Create
#Yourself #Change #Actions #Life #Gratitude

Feelings are one of the Ways Our Great Spirit Communicates
with us whilst in this Earth Realm.

Let Feelings Move You.

Listen to their messages.

Don't get Stuck in any Emotions they Create.

Release and Let the Emotions Pass Through.

Old Wounds and Hurts need to be Healed and Released.

Whether Joy or Sadness, Peace or a Storm, Everything comes from Love and is a part of our Growth.

Live, Love, and Surrender to Great Spirit.

#Feelings #Ways #Move #Spirit #Communicate
#Earth #Realm #Joy #Stuck #Emotions #Create
#Wounds #Hurts #Part #Healing #Release
#Sadness #Peace #Storm #Listen #Messages
#Growth #Live #Surrender

Our Journey here is not about Doing, it's about Becoming.

The Rose has no need to think about what it will become, it just grows from Deep Magic Within.

That magic and the Sun's power are creating an Unfolding of Promised Inner Blooms.

Life's Plan is Creating in Perfection.

Trust and Rest in Love's Light.

Your Magic is Unfolding.

#Journey #Doing #Become #Magic #Within #Sun #Power #Unfolding #Promise #Plan #Perfection #Life #Inner #Grow #Create #Trust #Rest #Light

We are Here to Remember
and Discover the Realm that We Came From, Love's Paradise.

Let's Join Hands and Hearts and Manifest that Paradise Again.

Stepping into Our Heart starts the process.

When we Sincerely Love, its Entrance is Revealed.

When we Make Love, we can Step in Together.

Love is Calling us Home.

#Remember #Discover #Paradise #Realm
#Hands #Heart #Process #Manifest #Entrance
#Reveal #Calling #Home

Take an Inventory of Beliefs.

Does Each Serve the You of Today?

Beliefs aren't Written in Stone, they are Just Thoughts, Repeated Many Times, that have become Neural Pathways, Habits of Thought, Now Called Beliefs.

Are they Yours or were they Inherited from Others for a Past Age?

Choose and Rewrite any that don't Support Your Current Life, Pleasure, and Purpose.

Repeat Your New Thoughts until they Overwrite the Old and Create Your Desired Outcomes and States.

#Inventory #Become #Thoughts #Outcomes
#Times #NeuralPathways #Belief #Habits #Past
#Rewrite #Repeat #States #Support #Pleasure
#Purpose #Desire #Create #Overwrite
#Others #Life #Serve #Today

Let Go of the Old,

**Sometimes going through the
Fire of Transformation is a part of
Our Process of Growth and
Awakening.**

**It's Our Misinterpretations, False
Beliefs, and Fears that are Burnt
in those Fires of Love.**

**It can Feel Painful, but the
Purging and Purifying is
Revealing the Fine Jewel We Are.**

**Open to the Light and Let
Love in.**

**The Joy of a New Morning is
Coming.**

#Fire #Transformation #Part #Process #Growth
#Joy #Awakening #Belief #Fire #Fear #Burn
#Purging #Purifying #Feelings #Open #Light
#LetGo #Pain #Reveal #Coming

Within Us is Also the Unknown.

Yet there is a Spirit Within that Knows All and Will in Time or out of Time Reveal All.

Ask to See beyond the Physical and Beyond Time.

We are Explorers and Can Look into the Mysteries of Life.

Love, through the Oneness, is Waiting to Reveal All.

Eventually, We will Know as We are Known.

Spirit is the Informer of All Things, Dare to Explore and Ask.

#Unknown #Within #Spirit #Know #Time #Reveal
#See #Beyond #Physical #Explorer #Look
#Mysteries #Life #Oneness #AllThings
#Dare #Explore #Ask

There is Magic in Acceptance.

**Acceptance of All Feelings,
even those that have been
pushed away.**

**Acceptance of All Sickness, if
it is in My World somehow it
is also in me.**

**Acceptance of All Sadness, if it is in
the World then it is also in me.**

**Acceptance of Our Many States can
Cleanse All.**

**The Magic is that Acceptance
brings Healing, Wholeness, and
Oneness Again.**

**Let Go and Let Love Bring Her
Powerful Magic and Reign.**

#Acceptance #Feelings #Magic #Sickness #World
#Sadness #Inside #States #Healing #Cleansing
#Wholeness #Oneness #LetGo #Powerful #Reign

When we Live in Light, it's Impossible to Reject Our Shadow.

Love, Even Our Shadow, Acceptance is the Key.

Too many feel the Shadow Self must be Overcome or Ejected.

Light Created and Reveals Our Shadows.

Knowing, even Our Shadow, is an Essential part of Our Oneness.

Find, Love, and Make Peace with Every Aspect of Self.

Loving, Even the Seemingly Unlovely Parts of Ourselves, is the Only Route to Our Happiness and Eventual Oneness.

#Light #Reveal #Shadows #Create #Knowing
#Live #Self #Feelings #Happiness #Part #Peace
#Impossible #Unlovely #Ourselves #Find #Key
#Oneness #SelfLove #Aspect #Acceptance

It's Impossible to Give Love Away.

In Spirit Love is Everywhere and Everything.

Sharing Love could be a better description.

It's only in our Minds Perception that we can Lose anything.

In the Realm of Spirit, Giving and Receiving are One, and there is Only Oneness.

Let Go of the Mind and its constant battle to understand.

Just Trust and Live in the Love You Are.

#Give #Receive #Spirit #Sharing #Realm
#Oneness #Mind #Perception #Impossible
#Constant #Battle #LetGo #Understanding
#Trust #Live

Sometimes it Seems Life has Different Ideas than Mine.

There doesn't Appear to be a Choice.

However, It's Best to Surrender to Life.

Deep Inside, there is a Knowing that I made the Choices before starting this Journey.

Now Life and Love are Carefully Guiding me towards my Ultimate Destiny.

My Mind tends to Protest, it feels it knows best, but Life says Trust.

Hold On, in spite of Seeming Appearances, Love's Triumph is Soon.

#Surrender #Life #Choice #Know #Journey
#Destiny #Mind #Trust #Care #Feelings #Inside
#HoldOn #Appear #Triumph

Become the Observer.

Are You Struggling with too many Thoughts?

Mind Chatter can lead on a Downward Spiral of Growing Confusion.

Overthinking and making Judgements, about every Action and Reaction, is constantly Stealing Peace.

Pause that Constant Whirring and Step into Heart Space.

Stop, Look and Listen.

There Spirit can Show the Solutions that Lead to Peace.

Let Love Guide.

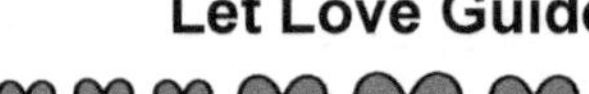

#Become #Observer #Mind #Thoughts #Lead
#Chatter #Struggling #Spiral #Grow #Confusion
#Thinking #Action #Judgement #Reaction #Heart
#Listen #Pause #Stop #Look #Spirit
#Peace #Guide

Do You Desire a Loving Relationship or Relationships?

Loving Yourself is the First Step to that Creation.

Without that Self-Love, Love can become Impossible to find.

Careful though, don't let it become Selfishness.

A Strange Truth, through Relationship, we can Learn about, and Discover Ourselves.

Healing Together is the Main Purpose of Spiritual Relationships.

Life's Lesson: Just Love, and Vibrate Love in whatever form or way Life Leads.

#Desire #Relationship #Learn #Without
#SelfLove #Find #Creation #Discover #Ourselves
#Truth #Healing #Life #Vibrate #Lesson #Why
#Yourself #Impossible #Care #Become

Sometimes it Seems Everything is Trying to Drag us Down.

Remember and Find Again, the Music of Our Soul.

Know Our Inner Being is More Powerful than any other source.

Rest in that place of Our Inner Heart, where Love's Music can always be Heard.

Deep Within, there is Peace, Inner Knowing, and Strength.

Have you Found that place?

#Music #Remember #Find #Soul #Inner #Know
#Being #Powerful #Source #Rest #Place #Heart
#Within #Peace #Strength #Found

There is a Step after Belief
on the Journey to Oneness.

Opening Our Heart fully will Lead
to Knowing.

Experience Living from the
Heart of Love.

We may not See it with our
Eyes as these are tuned to
Earthly Frequencies.

However, there is a place of Deep
Knowing, ready to be Discovered.
Have You found it?

In Our Heart, we Know as we are Known.

This is the Portal between the Realms.
For a while longer, we Live in both.

Knowing and Living fully in Our
Oneness is Our Home.

#Live #Knowing #Belief #Journey #Oneness
#Lead #Experience #Opening #Found #Heart
#Place #See #Eyes #Earthly #Discover
#Portal #Realm #Home

Looking for Love?

Find Love Within, then You will have Love to Share.

Love is best from a place of Giving.

It's impossible to Give without Receiving, though maybe, it doesn't always appear in expected ways.

Too many fall into the trap of Searching from a place of Hunger when there is so much Love to be found inside.

Explore, even through the rubble of Broken Dreams, Love is still there.

Love, Appreciate and Know that Our Return to the Oneness is already in Progress.

#Looking #Find #Share #Impossible #Ways
#Within #Give #Without #Receive #Appear
#Searching #Hunger #Found #Oneness #Inside
#Explore #Dream #Place #Appreciate #Know
#Return #Progress

I am not my Body.

I'm just Riding in this
Incredible Vehicle for a while.

Whatever happens to the Vehicle.

I am Forever Safe.

Enjoy this Earthly Ride, it's just
for a Short While, in the Grand
Scheme of Things.

We are Spiritual Beings
Exploring Life.

Be Sure to Leave all Weights,
and especially Fears behind.

When we Realise nothing can
Harm us, Deep Peace Abides.

Live Love Forever!

#Body #Vehicle #Forever #Safe # Life #Enjoy
#Earthly #Weights #Spiritual #Being #Explore
#Ride #Harm #Fear #Realise #Peace #Live

Have You Explored Your Breath?

Pause, Focus, and Slowly Breathe.

Take that Breath into the Centre of your belly, pause again, before slowly letting it out with a sound.

How does that Feel?

Repeat until you feel Centered and Calm.

Pure Magic, just from a few simple Breaths.

Explore the many types of Breathwork.

Focused breath will slow the chattering mind.

You can Ride Your Breath to take you to many realms and places of Ecstatic Pleasures.

#Now #Explore #Breath #Pause #Focus #Slow
#Chatter #Pure #Magic #Centered #Calm #Feel
#Feelings #Repeat #Ride #Places #Mind
#Realm #Pleasure

What Gets You Excited?

What Moves You?

What is Your Pleasure, and Brings Joy, Peace, Love, and Fulfilment?

Seek the Ways to Focus on these things.

Life is too Short to spend it all on Meaningless Drudgery and other Routines.

Live in Your Passion and Be the Love You Are.

#Excited #Move #Pleasure #Joy #Peace
#Fulfilment #Seek #Focus #Meaningless #Ways
#Drudgery #Life #Routine #Live #Passion #Be

Are You Your Own Best Friend?

How do you Treat the One you Spend the most time with?

Belittling thoughts, things that would never be said to another or especially children can, too easily, become Habits.

How about Changing those Patterns and Practising more Healthy Self Love?

Especially take some extra Care for your Inner Child.

Take the time to Love You.

Love will then Grow and Spread throughout Our World.

#SelfLove #Friend #Belittling #Children #Health
#Care #InnerChild #Become #Habits #Time
#Thoughts #Patterns #Practice #Growth #World

Maybe it's Time to Escape the Madness and Step Inside?

Or maybe just Laugh with the Dream.

Some still feel this is Reality!

Love says, Fear Not!

Awakening will come.

For Now, Live, Love, and Trust.

There is a different Realm where Our Heart Abides.

#Time #Escape #Madness #Inside #Dream
#Feelings #Reality #Fear #Awakening
#Now #Live #Trust #Realm #Heart

Searching for Love?

Where am I Looking?

Look Deep Inside, Step into the Heart, where Love Abounds.

Return to that Place of Being Pure Love, which cannot help but Attract more of it's Kind.

Becoming again, the Love that is Desired, this will Multiply and fill Our World. Our Root is Love.

Never Fear, Love is Calling us all Back Home.

#Searching #Looking #Inside #Heart #Return
#Place #Being #Pure #Help #Attract #Desire
#Becoming #World #Fear #Calling #Home

Remember there are Seasons
in our Earthly Experiences.

When it feels like all is Lost, when Dreams are failing, and Hope is slipping away. It's time to Notice that many Trees lose their leaves every year and Survive.

In fact, they usually come back with more Growth the following Spring.

Let Go of the Old, Hold On, and Trust, Knowing Your Time will come.

Winter's purging will soon be done. The Warmth of the Sun will Return, Your Fruitfulness and Growth will soon Prosper again.

Spring will soon return for us all.

#Remember #Seasons #Earthly #Experience
#Lost #Dream #Hope #Growth #Spring #LetGo
#HoldOn #Know #Feelings #Trust #Winter
#Time #Purging #Warmth #Sun #Return

Is Your Heart Open and Seeking?

Can You Let Go and Drop Into the Heart, Leaving Mind Chatter for Awhile?

Spirit is Waiting to Lead, Guide, and Help in Our Journey Back to Love.

Awakening to the Realm we Forgot for a Time is Coming for All.

That Forgetfulness is a part of the Dream.

What will I do in the Dream before the Choice to Wake up?

#Open #Heart #Seeking #LetGo #Mind #Help
#Chatter #Spirit #Lead #Guide #Journey #LetGo
#Awakening #Time #Coming #Forgetfulness
#Part #Realm #Forget #Dream #Choice #WakeUp

Be Aware and Notice Self-Talk.

Have Compassion, most
Voices originate from a part of
us that wants to keep us Safe.

Now, their advice may not be
so useful any more to the Adult
you have become.

Love and Reassure, they have
been heard and can now rest
and be Integrated again. Let
your Adult of today make the
Choices and Decisions
needed, not some echoes of
Past Programs.

We can Teach the Thoughts in our
Heads to work together in Union.

#SelfTalk #Voices #Aware #Compassion
#Choice #Become #Part #Programs #Union
#Today #Safe #Now #Past #Rest #Teach
#Work #Want #Thoughts #Head

There is a Purpose to this Life.

Have You Found Yours?

Awakening and Choosing Love is the Biggest Part.

We are each like Flowers connected on the Tree of Life, each with Different Gifts and Callings.

There is a Plan, which I Believe we Choose and Agreed, before this Journey.

Your Purpose and Calling will be Revealed in Due Time.

For Now, Explore Love, Loving Yourself, and All Others, then Watch that Life, Love, and Purpose Unfold.

Our Destiny and the Return to the Love We Are is Written in Our Hearts.

#Awakening #Purpose #Found #Choice #Part
#Life #Flower #Gifts #Plan #Reveal #Calling
#Connection #Agree #Journey #SelfLove #Now
#Believe #Explore #Yourself #Others #Watch
#Unfold #Time #Destiny #Return #Heart

Feeling Stuck in the Darkness?

Remember, the Light is Still on and Always ready to be Found.

Look in Your Heart.

Love is Ever Shining.

Even when seemingly Lost, in some Dark Night of the Soul, there are Glimmers of Hope to be Found.

Look for Love's Reflection, Shining through Others, or Messages of Hope in the Books of Love.

The Dawn is Coming. Hold onto the Love You Are.

#Remember #Feelings #Light #Stuck #Darkness #Found #Look #Heart #Shine #Others #Lost #Dark #Night #Soul #Hope #Messages #Dawn #Coming #HoldOn

What am I Thinking?

Would I Talk that way to Someone Else?

Change Your Thoughts, Change Your Life.

Are those Thoughts Uplifting and Positive, or Critical and Condemning?

Are they Loving and Kind?

We can, too easily, become our Own Worst Enemy!

Yes, Face the Facts. Yes, Let Emotions Flow, but face everything and every Voice with Compassionate and Understanding.

Self Love is a First Step to Changing Our World.

#Thoughts #Change #Life #SelfTalk #Positive
#Uplifting #Kindness #Become #Enemy #Way
#Emotions #SelfLove #Flow #Voice
#Compassion #Understanding #World

Love has Our Back.

We are Not in this Alone!

Our Higher Self, the Love we are, is working behind the scenes and will Succeed in the Ultimate Goal of Reuniting us all in Love.

Trust and Fear Not.

There are just a few steps further of Growth and Awakening.

Remember what we see with our Earthly senses can be the Opposite of Reality in the Spirit World.

Live Love and Watch with Expectations of Our Coming Triumphs.

#Alone #Self #Succeed #Reunite
#Trust #Fear #Steps #Growth #Awakening
#Remember #See #Senses #Reality #Spirit
#World #Live #Watch #Coming #Triumph

How can I Survive the Storm?

**Be Grounded, Be Centered,
Knowing, I am Not the Storm.
Trusting Love's Protection.
Knowing sometimes Storms are
Needed for Washing, Purging,
and Cleansing.**

**By Knowing All Things Change
and the Sun Will Shine Again.**

**Learning when to Hold on and
when to Let Go.**

**Know All Things work together
for Good for All who Love.**

**Most of All Trust and Know that
Love's Rainbow will soon return
and Shine again in Our Sky.**

#Storm #Grounded #Centered #Protection
#Trust #Washing #Purging #Cleansing #Return
#Change #Sun #Shine #AllThings #Work #Good
#Know #Learning #Rainbow #HoldOn #LetGo

Throughout your Day Today, Sow Love.

Do You Desire more Love?

Then Share more Love!

Share a Smile, a Gift, Words of Encouragement or Support, a Hug.

In the Realm of Spirit, in the Oneness, Giving and Receiving are One.

It's Impossible to Give without Receiving in some way.

Pay Attention to what you Give, be sure it comes from Love as it will Return.

Let's Sow more and more Love. The Day of Harvest is Coming.

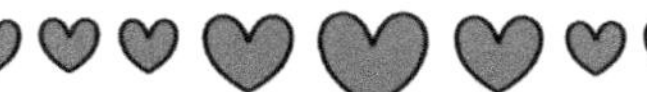

#Support #Sow #Smile #Gift #Encouragement
#Desire #Share #Hug #Impossible #Give #Way
#Without #Receive #Spirit #Attention #Return
#Oneness #Today #Realm #Harvest #Coming

Explore Being.

Move from the Realm of the Mind, and its Constant Babble of Thought, into the Heart-Space of Feeling.

Open to Experiences.

Let their Feelings Ripple throughout your Consciousness.

Let every Emotion flow through, without Judgement.

We are here to Explore, Experience, Love, and Enjoy.

Let Go of all Old Stories and Damaging thoughts.

This will help Create Heaven in Our Realm.

#Being #Thoughts #Feelings #Explore #Mind #Constant #Heart #Open #Experience #Flow #Consciousness #Emotions #Without #Judgement #Enjoy #LetGo # Move #Stories #Help #Create #Heaven #Realm

We have come to this Life to Experience!

We are Human Beings, not Human Doings!

Take the time to Love, Connect, Be Still, to do the things You Love.

Explore Nature, Different Cultures, and New Places. Discover your Passions and Pleasures.

This Life is too short to spend it all in Daily Drudgery.

Live and Share Your Love.

We are Heading Back to the Oneness.

#Experience #Life #Human #Being #Time #Doing #Connection #Discover #Nature #Passions #Still #Share #Places #Live #Pleasure #Drudgery #Oneness

Do You have a Dream?

Life may be short, Find the way to Make your Dream Happen.

Is that Dream Inspired by Love?

If so, Love will Open the Doors and Empower you in the Perfect Time.

Take the Steps one at a time and Watch the Way Open as you step out.

Be Bold, Be Brave, Be Alive.

Fears will Flee as you Start your Journey, and Love will hold Your Hand.

#Dream #Life #Find #Inspired #Open
#Empower #Time #Steps #Watch #Way #Open
#Fear#Perfect #Journey #Hold #Hand

There is always Light, Love, Encouragement, and Strength to be found, even in the Darkest moments.

The Question to ask is, where am I Looking?

What thoughts keep me from that Love.

It's time to Let Go of all the Old Stories, Old Patterns and Old Habits.

These things can keep us Stuck in the darkness.

Look to the Light.

Use the Power of Gratitude to melt the old.

Healing can be received in any Moment.

A New Dawn awakes.

#Light #Encouragement #Strength #Looking
#Ask #Time #LetGo #Stories #Patterns #Habits
#Stuck #Found #Darkness #Found #Power
#Gratitude #Question #Moments #Melt #Healing
#Thoughts #Receive #Dawn

We are all Artists, Playing, and Creating in many Realms.

What will you Create Today?

A Place of Peace, Connection, and Unity?

A Song of Love to Touch many Hearts?

**A Healing Prayer to Surround
Your World?**

**A Picture of the Love you are to Radiate
throughout the World?**

**A Vision to Inspire the Hearts of
those you Meet?**

**A Deep Love poured with Forgiveness
for Yourself and Others?**

**Your Place in the New World of
Your Dreams?**

**Create with Love in those Dreams, and
all will Manifest in Our World!**

#Play #Create #Realm #Place #Peace
#Prayer #Connection #Unity #Healing #Heart
#Picture #Vision #Inspire #Forgiveness #Meet
#Others #Yourself #Touch #Today #World
#Dream #Manifest

Our Experiences in this Life could be likened to Time in the Womb.

Some Mothers are not so Healthy, like the current state of Our Earth and its current systems.

Life can become difficult for the growing baby.

Some deliveries are not easy with mother and baby going through Trauma.

Trust, as we will all be Born into the New World that is Promised.

Life's Tests, Trials, and painful Growth will soon be forgotten.

There is Great Joy coming, when we will All Come Home to the Heart of Love.

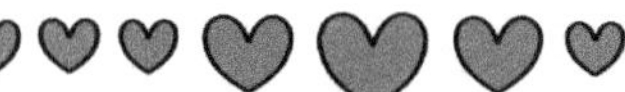

#Womb #Experience #Time #Mother #Health
#Earth #Become ##Difficult #Trauma #Trust #Joy
#World #State #Promise #Tests #Trials #Growth
#Pain #Forgotten #Life #Coming #Home #Heart

Much of our Journey Home is about Letting Go and Forgiveness.

Don't be Surprised when meeting what seems like the same Situations and Lessons over and over again.

Sometimes it takes a Deeper Look or a little more Letting Go to Undo the Power of Beliefs about Events or People who have shaped our Lives.

We Learn, Grow, and Change in Spirals of Progress.

The Deeper the Wound, the more Love and Attention it may need to Heal.

Enjoy the Journey and Trust. Wherever it takes you, Love is Guiding us Home.

#Spirals #Journey #Home #LetGo #Forgiveness
#Situations #Lessons #Look #Belief #Attention
#Healing #Events #Learn #Growth #Progress
#Change #Wound #Power #Enjoy #Trust #Guide

Take some Time Today to Be Still.

Go Inside, or Outside into Nature.

Stop, Look, and Listen.

Being too Busy is one of the curses of our modern life.

It's a strange Paradox that it takes Stillness to get into Flow.

Great Spirit is Calling Us into Oneness.

Step out of the Hustle and Noise of the Abnormal Life we have Created, Live, and Love.

#Still #Time #Flow #Inside #Nature #Today
#Stop #Look #Listen #Busy #Stillness #Life #Flow
#Spirit #Calling #Oneness #Create #Live

Let's Look for and Recognise the Spirit of Love in Every Human Being.

Sometimes it appears to be Buried quite deep, underneath Fears or the Rubble left from some of Life's Tough Experiences.

It's our Task, as Loving Explorers, to see past these Illusions and recognise our Oneness and any Mirrors or Learnings in each encounter.

Just Loving and Forgiving, even keeping distance, if needed, can bring about Healing for all. We can Return Our World to Love.

#Look #Recognise #Spirit #Human #Being #Fear
#Life #Experience #Explorer #See #Past #Illusion
#Oneness #Mirror #Learning #Encounter
#Forgiveness #Appear #Healing #Return #World

Beyond the Ego-Mind is a Place where Heaven Reigns.

Have You Found the Directions yet?

Let Go, Drop into Essence through the Portal of the Heart-Mind.

There, We are United with Love's Spirit.

Peace can Prevail in Our Heart, even in times of this World's confusion and failings.

Here is Our Refuge, where All are Safe.

Let's Meet in that Divine Place and Celebrate Love.

#Beyond #Ego #Mind #Place #Heaven #Reign
#Found #Direction #LetGo #Essence #Portal
#Heart #Spirit #Peace #World #Confusion #Times
#Refuge #Safe #Meet #Divine #Celebrate

As Children, we were Programmed with a set of Beliefs.

As Adults, many of those Beliefs still shape Our World.

Beliefs are just Thoughts Repeated over and over until they became Neural Pathways and the Habits that frame our lives.

Is it Time to Re-evaluate and Choose more Empowering Beliefs that suit us and Create Our Desired Life and Outcomes?

Let's Repeat the Thoughts and Affirmations that Create and Promote Experiences and the World our Heart Desires.

#Beliefs #Choice #Children #Heart #Programmed
#World #Repeat #NeuralPathways #Habits #Time
#Belief #Desire #Life #Outcomes #Affirmations
#Thoughts #Empower #Create #Experience

Remember to Look for the Light.

Even in Times of Great Darkness, there is always some Light to be Found.

During the Night, even the most Distant Stars shine and can be Seen.

Know that the Love in Us is that Light, and it's time to Shine.

Be the Light.

All Little Acts of Love and Kindness will Lighten our World.

#Look #Darkness #Know #Light #Found
#Night #Shine #Act #Remember #Kindness
#Times #World

Have You Discovered Our True Self, Our True Inner Being?

Away from the Ego Mind, through the Portal of our Heart-Mind, there is a Place of Oneness where the Divine Love we are can be Found.

Live from that Realm and the Haze of Life's Confusion will begin to pass and that Knowing of Our Immortal Being will bring Heavenly Peace.

#Discover #Find #TrueSelf #Inner #Being
#Ego #Portal #Heart #Mind #Place #Oneness
#Divine #Live #Realm #Found #Life
#Confusion #Knowing #Peace

After Discovering Our Heart of Love, the Next Step on Our Journey Home is Letting Go and Transforming Old Mind Patterns.

These Old Beliefs and Habits of Thought, that were mostly Imprinted in Childhood, they are not Ours at all.

When they pop up in our Consciousness, Recognise and Let them Go.

Don't feel bad the Patterns only surface, so they can be Released and Replaced.

Add New Beliefs and Practices that will Enhance your New Direction.
Live Love!

#Transform #Mind #Patterns #Discover #Heart
#Release #Journey #Home #Belief #Habits
#Thoughts #Recognise #Feelings #Imprint
#Childhood #Live #LetGo #Consciousness
#Practices #Direction

Take the Time to Explore Loving Yourself.

Make an Appreciation and Gratitudes list.

Eye Gaze in the Mirror, take a Walk in Nature, Stop, Breathe, and Meditate.

Pamper Yourself with some Extra Self-care or Favorite Pleasures.

If you don't Love and Look after Yourself, how can you Love another?

It's the Difference between Burning out and Burning Bright.

When we are Inspired and Centered, Love's Spirit can Flow.

There, Giving and Receiving become One.

#SelfLove #Explore #Appreciate #Gratitude
#Care #EyeGaze #Mirror #Nature #Become
#Breath #Meditate #Stop #Pleasure #Inspired
#Centered #Oneness #Yourself #Flow
#Spirit #Look #Burn #Giving #Receive

What will it take to Stop, Look Inside, and Listen?

Rushing through Busy days, Masking an Aching Hunger with Constant Activity or Empty Routine can Rob us of so many of the Joys of Life.

Look for, and Engage with those Nourishing Moments, and Deep Connection with Life, Love, and Our Nature.

Take the Time You Deserve to Refill from the Wellspring of Our Beautiful Heart.

#Stop #Look #Inside #Listen #Rushing #Busy
#Hunger #Constant #Action #Routine #Joy #Life
#Time #Moments #Connection #Nature #Heart

Let's take a Look and Recognise the Mirrors Around Us.

Some are sent to Help us Grow Love and Gratitude, Some to Expand Tolerance or Compassion.

Others are sent to Help us Make Peace with Our most Despised, or Hidden Parts.

Each comes from Love with their own Gift.

Let's be Open and Recognise the Gifts that Love brings, However they are dressed, they are all for our Growth and Healing.

#Look #Recognise #Others #Mirror #Help
#Growth #Gratitude #Expand #Compassion
#Peace #Hidden #Parts #Gift #Open #Healing

How Can I Tune with Love?

Step into the Grounded Centre of Our Being, Our Heart-Mind.

From there, Look at all People and Experiences through the Lens of Love.

Use Kindness and Understanding rather than Judgement and Self-righteousness.

See Life as a series of Mirrors that show the parts of Our Greater Self that may need Healing and Loving Attention.

Live in the Spirit of Kindness and Compassion, Loving all in the way I would like to be Loved.

#Grounded #Centre #Being #Heart #Mind
#Experience #Spirit #Kindness #Understanding
#Parts #See #Life #Judgement #Attention
#Selfrighteousness #Healing #Mirror #Self
#Way #Live #Look #Compassion

Let's Make Friends with Our Monsters and Melt their Powers Back into Love.

Fighting won't Work! Loving Will!

Each Part of Us is there for a Purpose.

Some Parts got left behind, after Guarding us from perceived Threats from when we were Young.

We have Outgrown those situations but forgot to Release and Thank them.

Let's Reconcile all our Parts, bringing each Part of us back into the Unity of our Oneness.

#Monsters #Friends #Melt #Power #Fighting
#Parts #Purpose #Growth #Release #Situations
#Work #Reconcile #Unity #Oneness

Each Moment I Have a Choice.

What will I Focus on?

What I Focus on Expands.

Even in the Darkest Moments, can I find a Glimmer of Joy and Happiness.

Yes, there are Times of Sadness, but be sure to let the Sun come out again.

It's too easy to get Stuck playing Old Tunes. Look for the Rising Sun and the Rainbow.

Forgive All concerned, and especially Self. Is it time to Choose Happiness Again?

#Happiness #Choice #Feelings #Focus #Expand
#Play #Dark #Moments #Find #Joy #Times
#Sadness #Look #Sun #Stuck#Rainbow
#Forgiveness #Self

We have an Inbuilt Homing Device.

It is set to Activate, at the Perfect Time, and to Guide us Back Home to Love.

When You Feel that Emptiness, that Longing, Rejoice, it's Love's Call.

Nothing can Satisfy that Hunger, except Reconnecting with the Love we are.

Listen to your Activated Heart.

It will Guide and Lead on Our Amazing Journey Back to Oneness.

#Longing #Home #Heart #Perfect #Time #Guide
#Feelings #Emptiness #Hunger #Reconnect
#Time #Rejoice #Listen #Lead #Amazing
#Journey #Oneness

It's Time to Close the Old Book
and to Stop Living in Past Disempowering Stories.

Write a New Book full of Pleasures, Desires, Possibilities, and Accomplishments that you'd Like.

Surely, by now, You and all Listeners must be fed up with that Old Disempowering Story?

Scratch the record, so it can't play any more or just Let it Go!

If you must tell the story one last time, write it down, then burn it!

Time has left it behind. You can too!

Write your New Story, then Watch it Unfold.

#Stories #Stop #Past #Now #Disempowering #Time #Pleasure #Desire #Possibilities #Burn #Accomplishment #Play #LetGo #Write #Watch #Unfold

Are You Loving Life?
Slow Down!

Take some Time to Appreciate Life's Little Gifts.

When did you last Stop and Smell a Rose?

Or Watch a Sunset or Sunrise?

Or to Share Words of Appreciation with a Loved One?

Stop, Breathe, Center, and Appreciate!

Life will Kiss you back with new Warmth and Meaning.

The not so merry go round of 'Normal Life' is spinning out of control.

Let's get off and Return to Love.

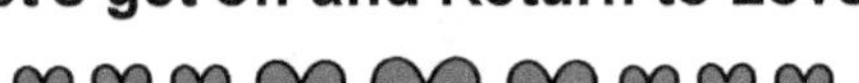

#Life #Slow #Time #Appreciate #Gifts #Stop #Breath #Centered #Share #Kiss #Warmth #Sun #Watch #Meaning #Normal #Control #Return

In Difficult Times, Self Care and Self Love are So Much More Important.

Take Extra Time to Relax and Enjoy, Seek the things that bring Pleasure.

Don't Drive your body and mind so hard.

The Love You are needs a Centered and Grounded Being to create Flow.

This way, we can Find Peace, even if Our Outer World is engulfed in Winters Storms.

There is Peace to be Found in the Center of Our beautiful Heart.

#Care #SelfLove #Time #Important #Relax #Enjoy
#Seek #Pleasure #Drive #Body #Mind #Centered
#Storms #Grounded #Being #Create #Flow #Find
#Way #Peace #Difficult #World #Winter #Outer
#Found #Heart

One Purpose of Our Journey here on Earth
is to Discover, Remember and Find Our True Self.

To Heal Past Wounds and Learn to Love Ourselves.

We can then also Discover Our Hidden Talents and use those Skills to Touch Lives and Change Our World.

Have you Found Yourself and Your Gift for Humanity?

#Purpose, #Journey #Earth #Discover
#Remember #Find #TrueSelf #Healing #Past
#Wounds #Learn #Ourselves #Hidden #Talents
#Skills #Touch #Change #World #Gift
#Found #Yourself

There Will Come a Day where there are No More Sorrows or Tears.

Joy will Reign in Love's Realm.

Now is the Time to let the Emotions Flow.

Let the Sorrow Wash Our Beautiful Heart, it will Cleanse the Hurts and Heal Old Wounds.

Seek not to Avoid the Call.

After the Fire and Purging, let those Tears wash you.

A New You is Growing Inside.

The Trials are Preparing us for a World where Love Reigns Supreme.

#Sorrow #Heart #Tears #Joy #Reign #Realm
#Time #Emotions #Wash #Flow #Cleansing
#Hurts #Healing #Wounds #Seek #Fire #Purging
#Inside #Grow #Trials #World

We are the Creators of Our Reality.

Are You Creating all You Desire?

Let's Remember our Power.

Get Centered and Grounded, then Drop into Our Heart, to be Sure all that is Created is Born from Love.

Our Power comes from that Place of Love.

Love and fear are the roots of all Actions.

Be Sure to Create from Love.

Have Patience, it can take a while for Seeds and Manifestations to Grow.

#Creator #Reality #Power #Desire #Remember
#Place #Centered #Grounded #Heart #Fear
#Roots #Action #Create #Patience #Seeds
#Manifest #Growth

Look Inside.

We are the Universe.

Realise the Amazing Wonder of You.

Billions of Living Cells working Together, Yet You are Greater than all these Parts.

Drop into the Heart-Mind and Discover our Truths, they are Waiting for you to Find.

Fall in Love with Our Magnificence and Celebrate.

#Truth #Look #Inside #Universe #Realise
#Amazing #Wonder #Self #Parts #Heart #Mind
#Discover #Find #Magnificence #Celebrate

Let's Seek and Find Gratitude and Acceptance for All the Gifts that Life Brings.

Even those that don't seem to be in line with our Choices or Ideal Experiences.

Maybe some are to find out what we don't want, to Empower Choice and New Directions.

One Day we will See and Understand how All of these things are a Blessing and a Part of Love's Growth on Our Journey Home.

#Seek #Gratitude #Acceptance #Gifts
#Direction #Choice #Experience #Find #Want
#Empower #Growth #Part #See #Understand
#Life #Journey #Home

Don't be Afraid to Cry, even Men,
for whom this can be a Taboo!
Let Go and Let Flow!
Crying is our Bodies Natural Release.
Emotions must Flow, or they can Create Lifelong Blocks.
Be Vulnerable, Share your deepest Heartcry with Trusted Friends.
Especially let all Emotions pass through.
Sincere Heartcry can and will Change Our Lives.
We are Energy in Motion.
Let it Flow!
Love and Healings come through the Washing of those Tears.

#Cry #Tears #Grief #LetGo #Flow #Emotions
#Release #Energy #Create #Blocks #Vulnerable
#Trust #Friends #Change #Share #Life
#Healing #Washing

Blocked Emotions Cause Dis-Ease.

There are many Powerful Emotional Release tools to use to keep Emotions Flowing.

As we Awaken, Life will often take us back to Old Patterns and Events so we can Let Go and Let Old Stuck Energies move on.

It's too easy to Feel something is Wrong with me at times like this.

Actually, it's time to Celebrate as Life's Cleansing and Healing Process is working Perfectly.

A New and Purified You will soon be Welcoming a New Day.

#Blocks #Powerful #Emotions #Cause #Disease
#Release #Tool #Flow #Awakening #Life
#Cleansing #Patterns #Events #LetGo #Stuck
#Feelings #Energy #Perfect #Time #Celebrate
#Move #Healing #Process #Purified

Our Journey through Life
will also contain
Disappointments and Trials.
These seemingly Unpleasant
Experiences are necessary
for Our Growth.

They can help to Move us
from Stuck Places and
Situations and get Energy
Flowing again.

Gratitude, Acceptance, and
Knowing when to Let Go will
set us Free and help
continue the Progress on
Our Journey Back to Love.

#Disappointment #Journey #Life #Trials #LetGo
#Unpleasant #Experience #Growth #Help #Move
#Stuck #Energy #Flow #Gratitude #Acceptance
#Situations #Places #Knowing #Free #Progress

Our Life Flows in Seasons.

Just as in the Physical World, Our Spiritual Life has times of Growth, times of Fruitfulness, times of Shedding, and times of Seeming Stillness.

Celebrate rather than Feeling bad when Seeming Loss or Trials come, or when the Spiral of Life takes us to Revisit Old Learnings in Deeper ways.

Trust! All things are Sent in Love to Guide us Home.

#Life #Seasons #Physical #World #Spiritual
#Times #Fruitfulness #Flow #Growth #Stillness
#Celebrate #Feelings #Learning #Trials #Spiral
#Ways #Trust #AllThings #Guide #Home

Look Inside.

I Am the Love I Seek.

Finding Our True Self, and Realising that there Within is Love which is the beating Shared Heart of Our Universe, that is a Huge Part of Our Purpose and Journey Here.

Celebrating that Love will Cause it to Flow out and Fill Our World.

All is Within that Oneness.

#Look #Inside #Find #Seek #TrueSelf #Within
#Heart #Universe #Purpose #Journey #Celebrate
#Cause #Flow #World #Within #Oneness

I Know Life Loves Me!

No Matter how things Appear, I Know All Things Work Together for Good for those who Love.

Sometimes the Elephant in the Room is no Bigger than a little Mouse, when we Open Our Eyes in Spirit and See what is Really Happening.

Trust the Love that has brought us this Far.

It will be with us Always.

After all, We Are That Love!

#Know #Life #Appear #AllThings #Work #Good
#Open #Eyes #Spirit #See #Trust

One Day we'll Understand.

Sometimes the Opposite of what Appears is what is actually Happening.

Our Physical Senses Perceive a Darkening World where our thoughts too often underline our failings.

Let's Remember Compassion and Self Love.

Our Growth here is about Loving and Caring, it's not about Results.

As we realise the Love we are, we will discover All Paths lead Home.

#Understand #Appear #Perception #Remember
#Senses #Dark #Physical #World #SelfLove
#Care #Compassion #Growth #Discover #Realise
#Thoughts #Results #Path #Lead #Home

Awakening can Start with the Realisation, This World is not where it's at!

This is getting easier to see as more and more of Normal falls apart.

Our New World of Love is just an Inner Change of Attitude and Beliefs Away.

Move from the Self Centered ego-mind into the Heart-Centered Realm of Connection, Oneness, and Love.

Realise, underneath all the mind games, we are Spiritual Beings making the Choices that will take us back on the route to Our True Home.

#Awakening #Realise #World #See #Connection
#Oneness #Normal #Ego #Mind #Attitude #Home
#Change #Belief #Heart #Realm #Self #Centered
#Games #Move #Inner #Spiritual
#Being #Choice #True

Our Hearts Communicate.

In Spirit, our Hearts are All One.

Our Heart Feels and Generates its Own Communications.

It Creates Love!

Our Heart-Mind is Our Connection with the Realm of Spirit and All Love.

Be Sure to Check in with Your Heart today.

#Heart #Feelings #Communicate #Oneness
#Create #Mind #Connection #Realm
#Spirit #Today

As in our Physical Bodies,
where muscles can get Tight and Cramp when misused.

Our Beings have places where Emotional Baggage has piled up and become Stuck.

Make a Commitment to work through these places.

Use the Balm of Loving Understanding and Gentle Touch to Release Past Traumas.

Seeing, Touching, Holding, Caring for the Unloved Parts until they Release, and the Energetic Charge Flows Freely Out.

Let's Become Clear Channels for Love to Move through.

#Physical #Place #Being #Emotions #Baggage
#Stuck #Commitment #Work #Understanding
#Touch #Release #Past #Trauma #Hold
#Care #Unloved #See #Clear #Flow
#Become #Energy #Move

I Believe We Planned this Life before We Landed Here.

Our Journey Back to Love is Assured.

Our Core Being Never Left That Beautiful Place.

Our Mind Just Chose to Wander Here for a While of Learning, Growth, Experience and Discovery.

All Roads Lead Home.

#Plan #Journey #Assured #Life #Core
#Place #Being #Mind #Learning #Growth
#Experience #Discover #Lead #Home

Peace is Possible,
Even in the Midst of a Storm.

See Past the Storm, Envision and Feel the Calm of Returning Peace.

Only the Energy of Love Lasts Forever.

Hold Tight to Our Beliefs, Our Ideals, Our Love.

We are Not Alone, there are Angels, Helpers, and Friends Cheering us on.

The Storm is Just a Swirling of Old Energies Passing through.

Let it Go, and Find Again Your Perfect Peace.

#Peace #Possible #See #Past #Storm #Vision
#Angels #Calm #Feelings #Energy #Forever
#Hold #Belief #Ideals #Passing #LetGo #Alone
#Helpers #Return #Friends #Find #Perfect

There is a Place of Knowing,

**of Remembering, a Place in the Heart
where Life's Mysteries become Clear.**

**It's way past Human Understanding
and Far from the Whirrings of the
Conscious mind.**

Listen! The Voice of Spirit is Calling.

**Find it, in the Quiet of Night, the Heart of
Nature, or in Moments beyond Mind.**

Be Open to its Vibrations.

Accept All the Gifts Life Brings.

**There are Gateways and Realms
beyond Physical Senses.**

**Love has many Signposts and
Guides for our Journey Home.**

#Understanding #Acceptance #Knowing #Clear
#Remember #Heart #Beyond #Home #Calling
#Human #Moments #Mind #Voice #Spirit #Nature
#Find #Past #Quiet #Vibrations #Gateway #Night
#Place #Mysteries #Gifts #Realms #Physical
#Senses #Signposts #Open #Listen #Life #Way
#Become #Guide #Journey

There are Two Beliefs that could Change our Whole World:

I Am Enough.

We are All One.

These are two of the most important Realisations on Our Path Back to Love.

How Would I Act if these Beliefs became mine?

What Do I Believe?

#Belief #Enough #Change #Whole #World
#Important #Realisation #Oneness #Path
#Believe #Act

Here is the Mystery.

We Live in the Heart of Love, Yet we Perceive a very Different World through our Minds.

The Journey Back, Awakening from Crazy Dreams, Letting go of old failures, Misperceptions, and everything that weighs down our Heart, can set us Free and Reveal once again our True Home.

Our Joyous Reuniting, and the Discovery of Our True Selves, Rooted in Love, this is our Purpose and Destination.

#Mystery #Live #Heart #Perception #World
#Joy #Mind #Journey #Awakening #Truth
#Home #Crazy #Dream #LetGo #Failure
#Free #Reveal #Discover #TrueSelf
#Reunite #Purpose #Destination

Who am I?

Have I yet Discovered my True Self?

I am a Part of the Divine.

Surely the Divine cannot be Split into Parts?

Then I must also be the Divine.

There is knowledge, and Beyond, there is Knowing.

Let me slip into, and Live in that Knowing.

Beyond Time, I am the Knowing.

There lives the Perfect and Coming Realm of Love.

#Discover #TrueSelf #Parts #Divine
#Know #Live #Beyond #Time #Perfect
#Coming #Realm

In Conclusion

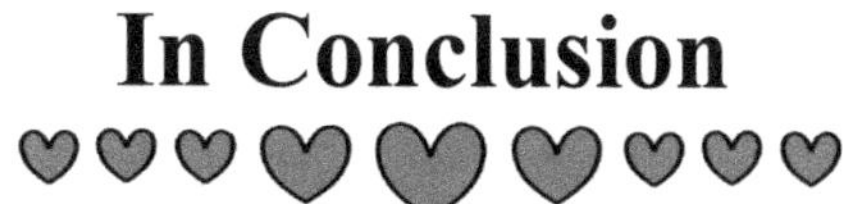

Thank You!

If you got this far, I trust you enjoyed the Messages.

Use it, Share it, and especially let the Quotes that speak to you become a part of your belief systems.

Words have Power and We become what we think about.

Use the Power of Repetition to let the Messages that Speak to you move you from head knowledge to Heart Knowing. Feel their Truths resonate, and let them build Your Faith and Trust in the Wonderful Power of Love to Create our New World.

Check out the Connections page, like and follow those pages to see Keith's posts and News of Workshops and Events.

The INDEX

Acceptance	5, 10, 26, 29,44, 49, 56, 76, 77, 128, 131, 141
Accomplishment	121
Act	2, 13, 111, 142
Action	20, 69, 80, 115, 126
Affirmations	6, 26, 54, 110
Agree	38, 40, 94
Alchemist	11, 28
All Things	2, 5, 16, 28, 31, 39, 61, 75, 98, 132, 134
Alone	97, 141
Amazing	46, 60, 120, 127
Angels	140
Animal	5
Answers	22, 24, 33
Appear	16, 35, 79, 84, 108, 134, 135
Appreciate	52, 84, 114, 103
Ask	17, 19, 20, 22, 30, 31, 35, 54, 75, 103
Aspect	5, 77
Assured	30, 139
Attention	37, 99, 106, 117
Attitude	20, 29, 136

Attract	69, 90
Automatic	3, 26
Autopilot	26
Awakening	47, 64,66, 74, 89, 92, 94, 97, 130, 136, 143
Aware	26, 93
Baggage	1, 12, 138
Battle	53, 78
Become	6, 15, 18, 34, 46, 55, 59, 69, 72, 74, 80, 81, 88, 93, 96, 105, 114, 138, 141
Being	6, 12, 14, 33, 35, 41, 43, 47, 52, 53, 56, 59, 68, 82, 85, 90, 100, 101, 108, 112, 123, 136, 138, 139
Belief	1, 3, 6, 8, 12, 26, 35, 42, 54, 61, 73, 74, 83, 106, 110, 113, 136, 140, 142
Believe	11, 19, 21, 39, 94, 142
Belittling	44, 88,
Beloved	18,
Beyond	17, 75, 109, 141, 144
Birthright	10
Blame	29
Blocks	129, 130
Body	6, 33, 85, 123
Boundaries	23, 48

Breath   17, 25, 47, 86, 114, 122
Burn   11, 74, 114, 121
Busy   53, 107, 115
Calling   7, 11, 37, 50, 58, 72, 90, 94, 107, 141
Calm   20, 86, 140
Care   79, 81, 88, 114, 123, 135, 138
Cause   5, 6, 20, 42, 130, 133
Celebrate   109, 127, 130, 132, 133
Centered   86, 98, 114,122, 123, 126, 136
Certainty   48, 51
Chakras   47
Change   1, 7, 8, 9, 13, 21, 42, 46, 54, 58, 63, 64, 69, 96,98, 106, 124, 129, 136, 142
Chatter   80, 86, 92
Childhood   12, 113
Children   3, 88, 110
Choice   3, 4, 6, 12, 26, 43, 45, 66, 79, 92, 93, 94, 110, 119, 128, 136
Circumstances   1, 9, 30
Cleansing   27, 57, 70, 76, 98, 125, 130
Clear   34, 138, 141
Comfort Zone   25
Coming   9, 10, 21, 64, 74. 92, 95, 97, 99, 105, 144
Commitment   138

Commune	24, 62
Communicate	70, 137
Compassion	44, 93, 96. 116, 117, 135
Confusion	62, 80, 109, 112
Connection	4, 31, 32, 36, 38, 45, 50, 55, 94, 101, 104, 115, 136, 137
Consciousness	29, 100, 113
Constant	34, 48, 53, 54, 78, 80, 100, 115
Control	12, 42, 48, 122
Core	12, 14, 139
Crazy	6, 143
Create	1, 2, 4, 5, 8, 15, 26, 31, 32, 42, 46, 51, 58, 60, 61, 63, 65, 69, 70, 71, 73, 77, 100, 104, 107, 110, 123, 126, 129, 137
Creation	4, 8, 10, 31, 39, 56, 81
Creator	4, 7, 126
Cry	129
Cycles	9
Dance	9, 47, 52, 55, 56,60
Dare	39, 75
Dark	10, 21, 24, 36, 67, 95, 103, 119, 135
Darkness	13, 95, 103, 111
Dawn	9, 21, 95, 103
Death	14
Decisions	93

Defeat   11
Design   4, 7
Desire   4, 5, 8, 28, 31, 35, 39, 51, 58, 61,
                      63, 69,73, 81, 90, 99, 110, 121, 126
Destination   12, 143
Destiny   1, 10, 30, 46, 48, 79, 94
Difficult   12, 105, 123,
Direction   33, 109, 113, 128
Disappointment   67, 131
Discover   41, 55, 59, 62, 65, 66, 72, 81, 82,
                      101, 112, 113, 124, 127, 135. 139,
                      143
Disease   130
Disempowering   8, 121
Divine   5, 11, 14, 22, 41, 52, 57, 68, 109,
                      112, 144
Divinity   66
Do   13, 39
Doing   7, 71, 101
Dream(s)   16, 21, 39, 67, 84, 89, 91, 92, 102,
                      104, 143
Drive   46, 123
Drudgery   87, 101
Drunk   18
Earth   28, 59, 62, 70,
Earthly   6, 28, 48, 53, 66, 83, 85, 91
Ego   109, 112, 136

Emotions   6, 49, 67, 70, 96, 100, 125, 129,
                        130, 138
Empower   3, 6, 12, 102, 110, 128
Emptiness   120
Encounter   56, 108
Encouragement   99, 103
Ending   34, 59, 66
Enemy   96
Energy   8, 14, 15, 19, 31,62, 69, 129, 130,
                        131, 138, 140
Enjoy   15, 85, 100, 106, 123
Enough   59, 142
Enter   19, 34, 68,
Entrance   72
Escape   89
Essence   28, 58, 68, 69,109
Events   16, 106, 130
Evolving   50
Excited   87
Excluded   56
Expand   23, 116, 119
Experience   1, 4-6, 12, 20, 25, 29, 39, 44. 47,
                        54, 58, 60-62, 68-69, 83, 91, 100-
                        101, 105, 108, 110, 117, 128, 131,
                        139
Explore   17, 25, 33, 35, 47, 75, 84-86, 94,
                        100-101, 114
Explorer   75, 108

Eye Gaze   114
Eyes   31-32, 83, 114, 134
Failure   15, 143
Fear   10-12, 14, 20, 32, 39, 45, 55, 74,
                  85, 89-90, 97, 102, 108, 126
Feelings   9, 19,27, 33, 43, 47-48, 56, 58, 64,
                  70, 74, 77, 79, 86, 89, 91, 95, 100,
                  113, 119-120, 130, 132, 137, 140
Fighting   118
Find   3, 7, 22, 25, 43, 57, 77, 81-82, 84,
                  102, 112, 119, 123-124, 127-128,
                  133, 140-141
Fire   11, 40, 74, 125
Flow   2, 6, 13, 19, 28, 31, 33, 47, 51, 64,
                  66, 96, 100, 107, 114, 123, 125,
                  129-133, 138
Flower   68, 94
Focus   4, 86-87, 119
Forever   2, 11, 14, 16, 33, 35, 41, 47-49, 53,
                  55, 58, 64, 85, 140
Forget   60, 92,
Forgive
Forgiveness   10, 14-15, 29, 36, 44, 56, 104, 106,
                  108, 119
Forgotten   35, 105
Found   2, 22, 24, 52, 55, 82-84, 94-95,
                  103, 109, 112, 123-124

Free	131, 143
Freedom	5
Frequency	69
Friends	88, 118, 129, 140
Fruit	43, 62
Fruitfulness	91, 132
Fulfilment	87
Future	55
Games	41, 136
Gateway	19, 141
Gifts	25, 65, 94, 99, 116, 122, 124, 128, 141
Give	13, 21, 38, 42, 44, 47, 78, 84, 99
Good	16, 98, 134
Gratitude	69, 103, 114, 116, 128, 131
Grief	67, 129
Grounded	98, 117, 123, 126
Grow	
Growth	2, 7, 16, 23, 29, 36,43, 70-71, 74, 80, 88, 91, 97, 105-106, 116, 118, 125-126, 128, 131-132, 135, 139
Grudges	36
Guide	22, 26, 30, 37, 42, 50, 80, 92, 106, 120, 132, 141
Habits	73, 88, 103, 110, 113
Hand(s)	72, 102
Happiness	45, 58, 77, 119
Harm	85

Harmony   31
Harvest   99
Hate   44
Head   6, 93
Healing   7, 19, 23, 27, 36, 38, 43, 45, 50, 57, 66, 70, 76, 81, 103-104, 106,108, 116-117, 124-125. 129-130
Health   88, 105
Heart   2-4, 9, 11, 17, 19, 22, 24, 31-35, 37, 39, 41, 48-50, 53, 56, 58, 63-66, 68, 72, 80, 82-83, 89-90, 92, 94-95, 100, 104-105, 109-110, 112-113, 115, 117, 120, 123, 125-127, 129, 133, 136-137, 141, 143
Heaven   45, 100, 109, 112
Help   7, 16, 30, 40, 54, 90, 92, 100, 116, 131
Helpers   140
Hidden   24, 31, 36, 43, 116, 124
Hold   2, 8, 31, 45, 53, 138, 140
Hold On   6, 9-11, 21, 67, 79, 91, 95, 98
Home   11, 19, 31, 37, 42, 45, 52, 57, 64, 66, 72, 83, 90, 105-106, 113, 120, 128, 132, 135-136, 139, 141, 143
Hope   67, 91, 95
Hug   13, 38, 99,

Human	5-6, 51, 57, 101, 108, 141
Hunger	84, 115, 120
Hurts	9, 36, 41, 70, 125
Ideals	140
Illusion	2, 32, 41, 48, 108
Imagination	39, 58
Important	7, 13, 29, 123, 142
Impossible	13, 38, 47-48, 77-78, 81, 84, 99
Imprint	54, 113
Indestructible	14
Inner	1, 5, 7, 16, 29-30, 58, 63, 71, 82, 112, 136
Inner Child	88
Inside	8, 22, 24, 30, 58, 76, 79, 84, 89-90, 107, 115, 125, 127, 133
Inspire(d)	64, 102, 104, 114
Intention	8, 46
Inventory	12, 73
Journey	6, 11, 25, 30, 40, 43, 62, 66, 71, 79, 83, 92, 94, 102, 106, 113, 120, 124, 128, 131, 133, 19, 141, 143
Joy	5, 33, 45, 52, 59, 67, 70, 74, 87, 105, 115, 119, 125, 143
Judge(ment)	14, 80, 100, 117
Key	29, 56, 77
Kindness	44, 96, 111, 117
Kiss	40, 122

Know(ing)	10, 13, 14, 30, 34, 39, 41, 43, 47, 51-52, 57-59, 67-68, 75, 77, 79, 82-84, 91, 98, 111-112, 131, 134, 141, 143-144
Lead(ing)	3, 5, 33, 45, 56, 61, 64, 65, 80-81, 83, 92, 120, 135, 139
Learn(ing)	34, 81, 98, 106, 108, 124, 132, 139
Lessons	43, 51, 81, 106
Let Go	2, 9, 14, 19, 27, 36, 51-52, 63-64, 74, 76, 78, 91-92, 98, 100, 103, 109, 129-131
Life	9, 12, 14, 16, 20-21, 25, 30-32, 36-37, 40, 42-43, 46, 51, 54, 60, 62-63, 66-67, 69, 71, 73, 75, 79, 81, 85, 87, 94, 96, 101-102, 105, 107-108, 110, 112, 115, 117, 122, 128-129-132, 134, 139, 141
Light	21, 34, 36, 40, 62, 65, 71, 74, 77, 95, 103, 111
Listen	3, 17, 30, 33, 37, 65, 68, 70, 80, 107, 115, 120, 141
Live	2, 9, 14, 23, 25, 39, 41, 53, 59, 64-65, 69-70, 77-78, 83, 85, 87, 89, 97, 101, 107, 112-113, 117, 143
Loneliness	45, 58,
Longing	120

Look	13, 16-17, 20, 22, 24, 30-32, 37-40 60-61, 68, 75, 80, 90, 95, 103, 106-108, 111, 114-117, 119, 127, 133
Looking	54, 84, 91, 103
Lost	67, 91, 95
Love	**All**
Madness	89
Magic	2, 13, 21, 27, 49-51, 55, 71, 76, 86
Magnificence	127
Manifest(ation)	28, 35, 60, 63, 72, 104, 126
Meaning	122
Meaningless	87
Meditate	19, 47, 114
Meet	104, 109
Melt	11, 52, 103, 118
Memories	15, 29
Mercy	
Messages	37, 71, 97
Mind	2, 31, 33-34, 48, 51, 53, 64, 66, 78-80, 86, 92, 100, 109, 112-113, 117, 123, 127, 136-137, 139, 141, 143
Miracle(s)	28, 46, 51, 53
Mirror	24, 108, 114, 116-117
Moments	20-21, 53, 103, 115, 119, 141
Monsters	118
Mother	105
Move	64, 70, 87, 100, 130-131, 136,138
Music	82

Mystery (ies)	17-18, 43, 68, 75, 141, 143
Nature	5, 11, 18, 33, 37, 62, 68, 101, 107, 114-115, 141
Neural Pathways	26, 61, 73, 110
Night	10, 67, 95, 111, 141
Normal	17, 25, 122, 136
Now	15, 26, 45,, 51, 55, 59, 89, 93-94, 121,
Observe(r)	6, 26, 33, 80
Obstacles	16
Oneness	2, 5, 7, 22-23, 27, 29, 31, 34, 41, 44-45, 50, 53, 55-56, 60, 66, 68, 75-78, 83-84, 99, 101, 107-108, 112, 114, 118, 120, 133,136-137, 142
Open	37, 51-52, 74, 92, 100, 102, 116, 134, 141
Opening	31, 83
Opportunity	9, 51
Others	6, 10, 12, 15, 36, 43-44, 49, 65, 73, 94-95, 104, 116
Ourselves	29, 44, 77, 81, 124
Outcomes	73, 110
Outer	1, 18, 56, 58, 63, 123
Overwrite	12, 73
Pain	74, 105
Paradise	10, 54, 72

Parents	3
Part(s)	5-6, 29, 41, 45, 47, 50, 53, 56, 60, 70, 74, 77, 92-94, 116-118, 127-128
Passing	14, 16, 140
Passion(s)	25, 87, 101
Past	1, 9, 23, 31, 41, 55, 73, 93, 108, 121, 124, 138, 140-141
Path	12, 34, 42, 45, 135, 142
Patience	126
Pattern(s)	8, 15, 26, 50, 52, 54, 88, 103, 113, 130
Pause	26, 33, 37, 80, 86
Peace	20, 29, 36, 48, 53, 58-59, 70, 77, 80, 82, 85, 87, 104, 109, 112, 116, 123, 140
Perception	61, 63, 78, 135, 143
Perfect(ion)	14, 15, 35, 42, 51, 60, 71, 102, 120, 130, 140, 144
Persistence	21
Physical	32, 35, 132, 135, 138, 141
Picture(s)	1, 15, 18, 24, 32-33, 57, 62, 104
Pilot	6
Place	19, 23, 25, 28, 34, 48, 51, 55, 64, 68, 82-84, 86, 90, 101, 104, 109, 112, 126, 131, 138-139, 141
Plan	10, 14, 42-43, 51, 54, 60, 62, 67, 71, 94, 139

Play   5, 41, 48, 104, 119, 121
Pleasure   73, 86-87, 101, 114, 121, 123
Poison   36
Portal   17, 19, 48, 83, 66, 109, 112
Possibilities   51, 121
Possible   1, 28, 39, 52, 54, 61, 141
Power   28, 35, 42, 43, 46, 49, 71, 103,
                        106, 118, 126
Powerful   4, 19, 23, 27, 76, 82, 130
Practice(s)   26, 61, 88, 113
Prayer   19, 104
Problems   5-6
Process   51, 60, 72, 74, 130
Programmed   110
Programs   3, 93
Progress   29, 84, 106, 131
Promise   10, 71, 105
Protect   3, 41
Protection   98
Pure   11, 14, 40, 446 88, 90
Purging   40, 74, 91, 98, 125
Purify(ied)   11, 130
Purifying   40, 74,
Purpose   24-25, 43, 60, 73, 81, 94, 118, 124,
                        133, 143
Quest   34, 62
Question   19, 22, 26, 33, 103

Quiet	141
Rainbow	98, 119
React(ion)	20, 80
Realise	40, 85, 127, 135-136
Reality	4, 41, 61, 89, 97, 126
Realm	2, 14, 17, 25, 32, 34, 37, 45, 48, 59, 70, 72, 78, 83, 86, 89, 92, 99-100, 104, 112, 125, 135, 137, 141, 144
Receive	22, 38, 78, 84, 99, 103, 114
Recognise	5, 52, 54, 56, 108, 113, 116
Reconcile	29, 118
Reconnect	29, 50, 120
Recurring	54
Refining	40
Refuge	109
Regret	29, 55
Reign	27, 53, 76, 109, 125
Rejoice	51, 120
Relationship	7, 23, 31-32, 45, 50, 81
Relax	46, 123
Release	1, 8, 40, 49, 70,113, 118, 129-130, 138
Remember	9, 14, 32, 34, 66, 72, 82, 91, 95, 97, 111, 124, 126, 135, 141
Repeat	26, 73, 86, 110
Resentments	9

Resources	16, 36, 58
Responses	20, 26
Responsible	56,
Rest	19, 48, 51, 71, 82, 93
Results	135
Return	1, 9-10, 31, 40, 45, 67, 84, 90-91, 94, 98-99, 108, 122, 140
Reunite	49, 60, 97, 143
Reveal	31, 72, 74-75, 77, 94, 143
Review	36
Rewire	61
Rewrite	3, 26, 73
Ride	2, 66, 85-86
Rise	11, 40, 67
Roots	62, 126
Routine	25, 87, 115
Rushing	115
Sadness	27, 45, 70, 76, 119,
Safe	58, 85, 93, 109
Searching	84, 90
Seasons	91, 132
See	18, 31, 37, 52, 67, 75, 83, 97, 108, 117, 128, 135-136, 138, 140
Seed(s)	16, 28, 46, 62, 126
Seek(ing)	22, 48, 57, 65, 87, 92, 123, 125, 128, 133

Self	7, 15,36, 44, 52, 57, 66, 77, 97, 112, 114, 117, 119, 123-124, 133, 135-136, 144
SelfLove	7, 44, 81, 88, 114, 123, 135
Selfrighteousness	117
SelfTalk	93
Senses	17, 37, 97, 135, 141
Separate (ion)	31, 41, 45, 53
Serve (ice)	1, 3, 7, 12, 26, 54, 73
Shadows	5, 77
Shame	29
Share (ing)	2, 7, 13, 23, 33, 38, 55, 59, 65, 68, 78, 84, 99, 101, 122, 129
Shine	13, 24, 65, 95, 98, 111
Shrinking	25
Sickness	27, 43, 76
Signposts	33, 59, 141
Signs	18, 24, 62
Situations	26, 106, 118, 131
Skills	124
Slow	47, 86, 122
Smile	13, 55, 99
Sorrow	49, 125
Sorry	56
Soul	82, 95
Source(s)	22, 24, 82
Sow	99
Spiral	80, 106, 132

Spirit   17, 22, 30-31, 36, 45, 47-48, 50-51,
                     64, 70, 75, 78, 80, 92, 97, 99, 107-
                     109, 114, 117, 134, 137, 141
Spiritual   81, 85, 132, 136
Spring   91
State(s)   10, 27, 47, 49, 53, 58, 73, 76, 105
Steps   34, 39, 97, 102
Stop   17, 37-38, 44, 98, 80, 107, 114-115,
                     121-122
Storm(s)   9, 16, 58, 70, 98, 123, 140
Story (ies)   10, 100, 103, 121
Strength   16, 82, 103
Struggle (ing)   48, 63, 66, 80
Stuck   6, 8-9, 49, 70, 95, 103, 119, 130-
                     131, 138
Succeed   97
Sun   9, 62, 67-68, 71, 91, 98, 119, 122
Support   30, 73, 99
Surrender   70, 79
Talents   124
Teach(ers)   59, 93
Tears   49, 57, 125, 129
Temporary   2, 16, 31
Tests   105
Thinking   4, 54, 80
Thoughts   42, 52, 54, 64, 69, 73, 80,88, 93,
                     96, 100, 103, 110, 113, 135

Time(s)   2, 7, 13, 15, 19, 25-26, 32, 36, 38-
                           39, 41-42, 45, 49, 56 58-59, 61, 64,
                           66-67, 73, 75, 88-89, 91-92, 94,
                           101-105, 107, 109-111, 114-115,
                           119-120-123, 125, 130, 132, 144
Today   3, 8, 13, 26, 56, 68, 73, 93, 99,
                           104, 107, 137
Tool(s)   4, 130
Touch   38, 49, 65, 104, 124, 138
Transformation   8, 74
Trauma(s)   1, 66, 105, 138
Trials   40, 105, 125, 131-132
Triumph   10, 79, 97
Trouble(d)   9, 16
True   15, 35, 50, 55, 136, 143
TrueSelf   19, 44, 52, 57, 66, 112, 124, 133,
                           143-144
Trust   14, 16, 46, 51, 60, 67, 71, 78-79,
                           89, 91, 97-98, 105-106, 129, 132,
                           134
Truth   15, 18, 21, 24, 32-33, 37, 41, 59-
                           60, 81, 127, 143
Unaccepted   56
Unconditional   57
Understand(ing)   33, 43-44, 62, 78, 96, 117, 128,
                           135, 138, 141
Unfold(ing)   42, 46, 60, 71, 94, 121
Unity   104, 118

Universe   35, 55, 60, 127, 133
Unknown   51, 68, 75
Unloved   138
Unlovely   77
Unpleasant   131
Uplifting   96
Vehicle   85
Vibrate (ing)   54, 69, 81
Vibrations   141
Victory   53
Vision   31, 104, 140
Visualisation   58
Voice(s)   30, 37, 93, 96, 141
Vulnerable   129
Wake Up   92
Walls   41, 49
Want   39, 43, 65, 93, 128
Warmth   91, 122
Wash(ing)   15, 45, 49, 57, 98, 125, 129
Watch   17, 30, 33, 46, 62, 94, 97, 102,
                  121-122
Way(s)   1, 3, 7, 17, 38-39, 61, 64, 70, 81,
                  84, 87, 96, 99, 102, 117, 123, 132,
                  141
Weights   36, 85
Whole   41, 50, 142
Wholeness   27, 29, 76

Winter	9, 91, 123
Wisdom	22, 64
Within	1, 17-18, 22, 24, 41, 48, 52, 56, 59, 62, 65, 71, 75, 82, 84, 133
Without	1, 13, 38, 81, 84, 99-100
Womb	105
Wonder(s)	23, 50-51, 55, 127
Work(s)	1, 7, 9, 16, 49, 51, 63, 93, 98, 118, 134, 138
World	1-5, 7-8, 13, 18, 24, 27-28, 31-33, 35-36, 46, 54, 56, 58, 61, 63, 65, 68, 76, 88, 90, 96-97, 104-105,108-111, 123-125, 132-133, 135-136, 142-143
Wound(s)	20, 41, 45, 70, 106, 124-125
Write	39, 121
Yourself	2, 10, 14, 16, 18, 52, 69, 81, 94, 104, 114, 124

About the Author

♥ ♥ ♥ ♥ ♥ ♥ ♥ ♥

Keith Higgs has lived an interesting and exceptional life.

A hippie search for truth; twenty years of International Christian-based voluntary work; Editing and publishing talks and inspirational audios; Building a successful computer business—then watching it crash; Two marriages, eight children and six stepchildren; Building a MLM business, Learning from the masters of personal growth; Attending and

assisting at talks and workshops; Studying NLP, healing and speaking skills; Building a social media platforms of thousands; Travelling many countries.
His combined skills, common sense, learnings and accumulated wisdom have flowed into:

"Take Control of Your Spacecraft and Fly Back to Love - A Manual and Guidebook for Life's Journey"

"The Little Book of Love - Quotes to Empower Your Journey Back to Love"

""Love, Sex, Nakedness and the Divine - Messages from Love to Empower and Enlighten Your Journey"

And Now, Posting Empowering Messages on Facebook nearly every day for over 3 years led to his latest books:

"Getting to the Heart of Love - 365 Quotes from Love to Encourage and Empower"

"Messages from the Heart of Love – Spirituality Basics in 144 Empowering Quotes"

Here is a man who has lived and learnt. He has a passion to share his truths, values, and beliefs with many.

Contact Keith for Speaking or Workshop Bookings

Website: www.KeithHiggs.com

Email: Keith@FlyBacktoLove.com

My Facebook pages:

facebook.com/KeithHiggs1

facebook.com/MessagesFromtheHeartofLove

facebook.com/GettingtotheHeart.info

facebook.com/LSND.info

facebook.com/TakeControlofYourSpacecraft

facebook.com/TheLittleBookofLove.info

Please add a like these pages. If you Loved the book, a review on Amazon, or other sites could help others to find it.

My author, books and blog sites:

www.KeithHiggs.com

www.FlyBacktoLove.com

Please join my mailing list to stay in touch.

I'm the administrator of a Facebook group 'Awake Your Dreams.' You may like to join us there. It is full of inspiring Quote pictures

www.facebook.com/groups/AwakeYourDreams

Please follow:

www.instagram.com/Keith_Higgs_FlyBacktoLove

OTHER BOOKS BY KEITH HIGGS

Take Control of Your Spacecraft and Fly Back to Love

Is a Guidebook and Manual for Love's Journey of Personal Growth and Spirituality. It has many stories, tips, and tools to help you take back control and let your journey become a smoother ride.

The Little Book of Love

It's a Little Book full or the most Inspiring messages and Powerful Quotes from the 1st Book, "Take Control of Your Spacecraft and Fly Back to Love - A Manual and Guidebook for Life's Journey"

Getting to the Heart of Love

365 Empowering Quotes, Messages from Love.

Words of Power can cut through fears and bring healing and growth, especially when repeated as positive affirmation.

Pick a message for the day or just open randomly any time of day for Inspiration.

Love, Sex, Nakedness and the Divine

It's a strange and sad thing that these words have had their meanings corrupted, denigrated and many taboos attached. Warning bells ring, yet desire is also aroused within to find out more.

The book looks at these in their purity, using inspiring messages. We can see how better attitudes to these topics can set us free, bring pleasure and even enlightenment.

To Get Your Paperback copies, eBooks or Audio Books.

Visit www.FlyBacktoLove.com

All of Keith's Books are available through his website. There you can read many parts of his books for **FREE**.

A free explorer membership of the interactive website is available to give a good taster of the books. There is also a **GOLD** membership option for just £10 to read, listen to, or download the first book and get a free eBook version of 'The Little Book of Love'.

Copies can be purchased through the site or through Amazon, Audible or any good online bookshop.

A request: If you are in the UK please use the Website to support the author. For orders outside the UK when considering the international postage, it's usually cheaper to buy through an online bookshop.